THE NEW PASTA COOKBOOK

JOANNE GLYNN

BayBooks
An imprint of HarperCollins*Publishers*

A Bay Books Publication

Bay Books, an imprint of
HarperCollins*Publishers*
25 Ryde Road, Pymble, Sydney, NSW, 2073, Australia
Distributed in the United States of America by
HarperCollins Publishers
10 East 53rd Street, New York NY 10022, USA

First published in Australia in 1988
Revised edition published in Australia in 1992
This edition published in the USA in 1995

ISBN 1 86378 250 8

Photography: Ashley Barber
Food styling: Michelle Gorry
Front cover photograph by Rowan Fotheringham with styling
by Donna Hay
(Spicy Ricotta Agnolotti in Herb Leaf Pasta, recipe on page 58; plate
supplied by Corso de Fiori, Darlinghurst, Sydney, 2010, Australia)
Printed in China
5 4 3 2 1
98 97 96 95

CONTENTS

~

THE PASTA STORY

Pasta's popularity has always been its adaptability. It can come in many different forms, with taste differences and visual variety; it is cheap, quickly and easily prepared; it can be a meal in itself or eaten with other foods such as meat and vegetables. Pasta has a high nutritional value and is an easily digested source of energy.

Pasta is a dough made from flour, water and/or eggs. The flour used for commercial pasta is made from milled durum wheat in the form of semolina, a coarsely ground meal. Dough made from durum wheat semolina absorbs less water and will dry easily; holds together well during kneading, drying and cooking; withstands pressure well; has a better texture and 'bite' and reheats successfully.

Eggs are sometimes added to commercial dried pasta to give extra body and flavor. Homemade pasta nearly always uses eggs which give the dough flavor and make it manageable and easy to roll.

BUYING PASTA

Bought pasta falls into three main categories:

PACKAGED DRY PASTA (*pasta secche*) which is available from every supermarket shelf. It is worth checking the labels to establish that durum wheat semolina has been used (*pasta di semolina digrano duro* on Italian imports) and for the use or exclusion of egg (*all' uovo* means with eggs). Cooking time for this pasta is 10 minutes or more as it needs to re-hydrate as well as cook.

FRESH PASTA (*pasta fresca*) is available from specialty pasta shops or gourmet shops and in the refrigerator case in supermarkets. It is often displayed in bulk and you can purchase as little or as much as you need. This pasta is quite pliable and takes only 1½ to 3 minutes to cook.

DRIED, PRE-PACKED 'FRESH PASTA' falls between the other two categories and is available from supermarkets and gourmet shops. Cooking time is 3 to 5 minutes.

HINTS ON COOKING

The success of a pasta dish depends on the correct cooking of the pasta you have chosen to use.

The proportion of water to pasta is important. Too little, and the pasta will be crowded and unable to cook evenly. It will go gluey as the relatively small amount of water becomes starch laden. There can never be too much water. Use a minimum of 4 quarts water to every pound of pasta; use more if cooking dried pasta, as it absorbs more water.

Use a very large pot. Bring the water to a rolling boil. Just before putting in the pasta add a dash of oil (to help prevent sticking) and, if desired, a large pinch of salt (Kosher salt or unrefined sea salt is good) which helps bring out the flavor. If using fresh pasta, shake it gently to loosen the strands before adding it to the water.

Once the pasta is in, stir to move it off the bottom of the pot. When the water comes back to the boil start timing, maintaining a slow rolling boil. Don't stir too often now as this tends to release excess starch.

The pasta is done when it is *al dente*: tender, but with some resistance to the bite. You should feel the texture and form in the mouth, not mushy dough. Moreover, if the pasta is overcooked it cannot physically support the rest of the ingredients and won't allow for an even distribution of the sauce. Taste the pasta just before the time is up. Note: As fresh pasta takes only a couple of minutes to cook, its timing is more critical.

Don't be over zealous in draining, as it is desirable to leave a little of the cooking water to help prevent sticking. Only rinse if the pasta is intended to be used as a cold dish.

Next, stir through a little oil or melted butter. This helps with the final saucing and stops the pasta sticking together. And, always have the waiting bowls and serving dishes warmed.

HOMEMADE PASTA

Plain flour is usually used when making egg pasta. It gives a fine textured, light dough which is well suited to filled pastas such as ravioli, as it gives the pasta good elasticity.

The addition of durum wheat semolina gives a better color, more flavor and a resilient texture, as well as providing the nutritional benefits of hard wheat flours. The proportion of semolina to plain flour is a matter of choice but a maximum of two-thirds semolina and one-third plain flour is recommended. In making pasta with other flours such as whole wheat or buckwheat, this point should be kept in mind as different meals and grains have differing absorption levels and 'short' qualities.

Eggs should be the freshest available, as their freshness not only influences the flavor and color of the pasta, but also the elastic quality of the dough.

The standard proportion of eggs to flour is 1 medium egg to every ¾ cup flour, and a pinch of salt is generally added. It is sometimes necessary to use a little water, but this will depend on the particular flours used and the humidity at the time. Eggless pasta is made the same way as egg pasta except that the eggs are replaced in volume by water.

The only equipment you need is a board or marble and a long rolling pin. However, a food processor takes the labor out of mixing, and a pasta machine simplifies and takes the guesswork out of rolling and cutting.

For a basic dough, you need 2 cups sifted flour, 2 eggs, a large pinch of salt and some water. This amount is enough to serve two main courses or three appetizers.

MIXING BY HAND Use a pastry board or a large bowl. Put flour in a mound with a well in the center. Add eggs and salt, and start blending with a fork or fingers, incorporating more and more of the flour into the eggs and working from the inside outward. When flour and eggs are combined, start to knead the dough on the board incorporating extra flour or adding water as necessary.

It will take about 5 minutes to get a smooth, firm dough. If durum wheat semolina is used, allow a good 7 to 10 minutes of kneading. It takes this time for the hard semolina to absorb moisture and develop its strong, pliable characteristics.

Only experience can tell you when the dough is ready. It should not be sticky or wet to the touch. If you can knead it well without adding flour, it is probably ready.

When finished, cover the dough with a damp cloth, plastic wrap or an upturned bowl to prevent a crust from forming, and rest it for at least 15 minutes.

MIXING IN A PROCESSOR Fit the metal blade. Add dry ingredients to the bowl. With the motor running, add eggs through the feed tube. After 5 seconds a ball should form. If the dough is still sticky, add flour until a ball forms, or the machine slows down or stops. Alternatively, a few drops of water may be necessary to take the dough from the meal stage. Take the dough out and knead it until elastic, 2 to 3 minutes. Rest dough as above.

ROLLING AND CUTTING BY HAND Divide the dough into manageable balls and keep them covered until needed. Working piece by piece, press out the center with your hand. Using a long rolling pin, roll each evenly and smoothly with a little flour on the board.

Lift and turn the dough often, and don't be in a hurry; you want an even, thinly rolled sheet of pasta. The pasta will swell a little with cooking, so roll it thinner than the desired cooked thickness. For filled pastas the dough should be next to paper thin.

When you're happy with the proportions, cover each sheet with plastic wrap or waxed paper, and then the lot with a dampened dish towel to prevent drying out.

If the dough is to be cut into strips like tagliatelle, let it rest to dry slightly; this prevents the ribbons from sticking together. Then cut the sheets into rectangles approximately 10 inches long and roll these up, along their length. Using a sharp knife and with smooth strokes, cut uniform slices which when unrolled become, for example, tagliatelle (¼ inch wide), pappardelle (⅜ inch wide) or whatever pasta type you decide to make.

ROLLING AND CUTTING WITH PASTA MACHINE Starting with the rollers on the widest setting, roll a flattened ball of dough through two or three times. Fold the dough in thirds and roll again. Repeat this process four or five times or until the dough is a smooth and elastic sheet of even proportions. Now pass the dough through the rollers setting them at decreasing widths apart, until the desired thickness is reached. Avoid adding flour. If dough becomes sticky, a light dusting should help it through.

If, before cutting, the dough seems too wet, let it sit uncovered for 15 minutes or so. It should be dry enough so that the cut lengths won't stick together but will still pass through the cutters without cracking. Crank the sheets of dough through the required cutting rollers.

Spread the cut lengths on plastic wrap, or hang them over the backs of chairs or a broom handle until

Try a combination of semolina and flour.

Making your own pasta is easy and fun.

ready to cook. Pasta made entirely with plain flour doesn't dry well; it tends to crack as the moisture evaporates.

MAKING FILLED PASTA The thinly rolled sheets should be kept under a damp dish towel or plastic wrap and used quickly.

Have the filling ready before the pasta so that you're ready to go as soon as the dough is made.

There are three main ways of making filled shapes:
i) Using a Mold: these are trays pressed with the grooves and ridges of different shaped and sized ravioli, which usually come with their own little rolling pin to seal and cut the dough around the filling. They are useful when a uniformly sized and cut pasta is desired.
ii) Sheeted Filling: this is a successful way of making many ravioli quickly. Cut two sheets of dough, one slightly bigger than the other. On the small sheet place spoonfuls of filling at even intervals, then brush along the intended cutting lines with beaten egg. Position the larger sheet of pasta over the top neatly and run over the cutting lines with your finger to make sure that both sheets of pasta are touching together. Now cut the shapes out with a floured pastry wheel. The best one to use is a cutter/crimper which cuts and seals at the same time, but a fluted or ravioli wheel is also effective. In a pinch, use the tines of a fork.
iii) Folded by Hand: this method gives a well-sealed ravioli as each one is pressed together by hand.

Working one sheet of pasta at a

Roll out pasta smoothly and evenly with a rolling pin.

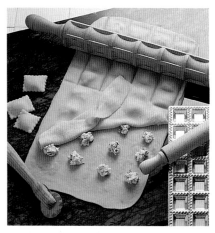

Special pasta making equipment makes the task easy.

time, cut out the shapes required (round for a half-moon ravioli; squares for triangles; rectangles for squares) and brush the borders with beaten egg.

Place a spoonful of filling to one side of the centerline of each. Fold the dough over the filling to match corresponding edges, press between the fingers and then seal the cut edge with a pastry cutter.

Place finished stuffed pasta on a tray or plate dusted with semolina or cornmeal and store in the refrigerator before cooking.

Dried Pasta available in more shapes and sizes than there are days of the year — rings for soups, rolled sheets for baking dishes, large shells for stuffing and all those long lengths for tempting sauces.

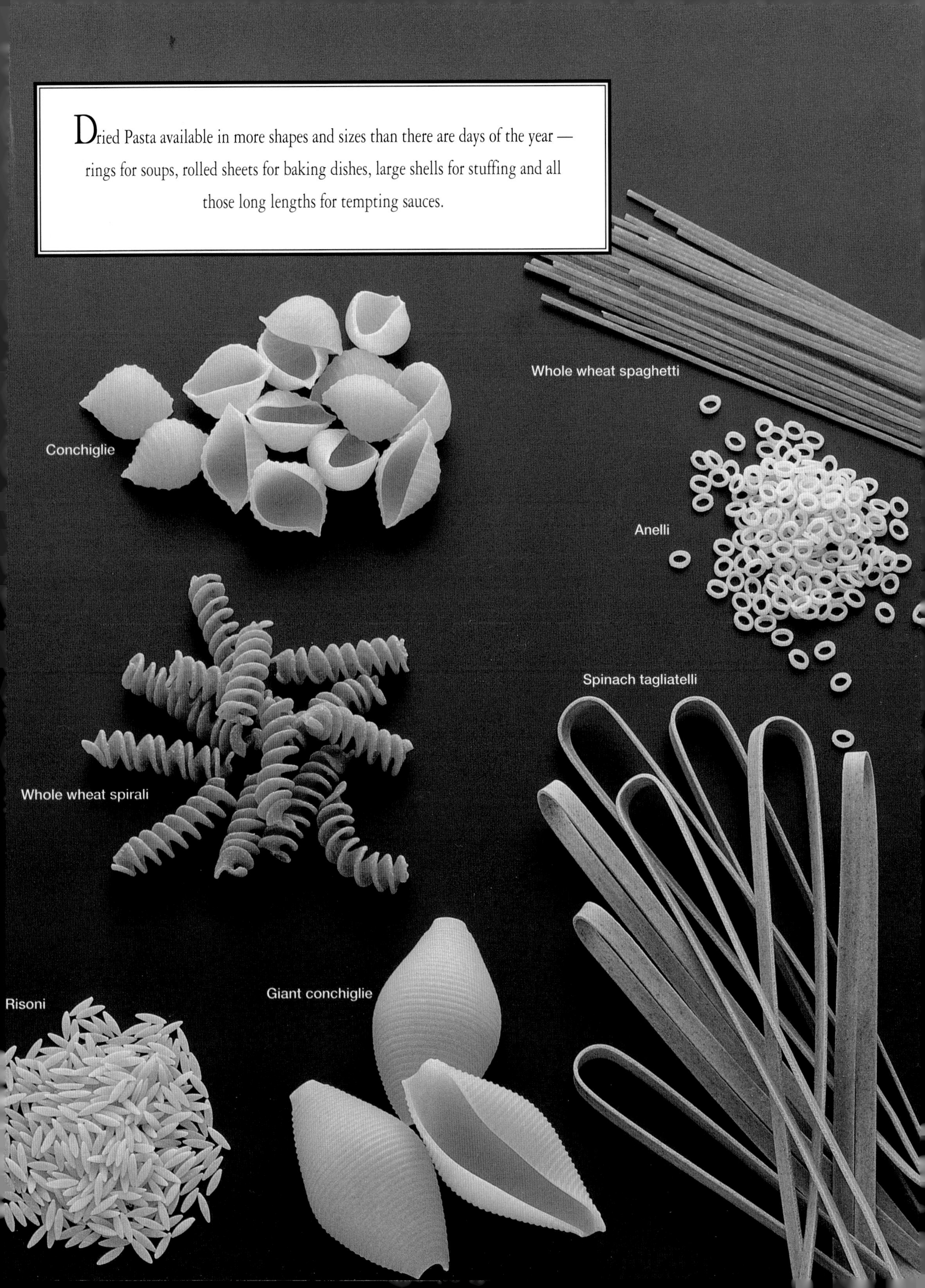

Whole wheat spaghetti

Conchiglie

Anelli

Spinach tagliatelli

Whole wheat spirali

Risoni

Giant conchiglie

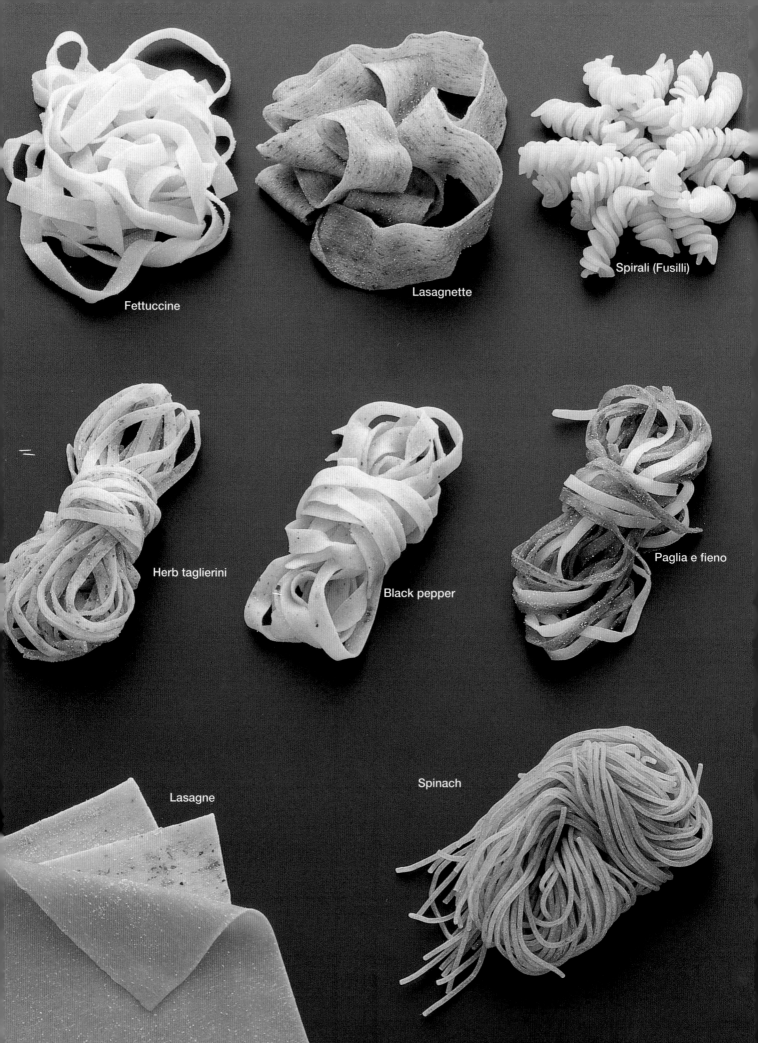

Fettuccine

Lasagnette

Spirali (Fusilli)

Herb taglierini

Black pepper

Paglia e fieno

Lasagne

Spinach

Fresh Pasta — for taste, texture, temptation.
Today an integral part of a truly balanced diet.
Cooks in minutes for that minimum effort maximum result meal.

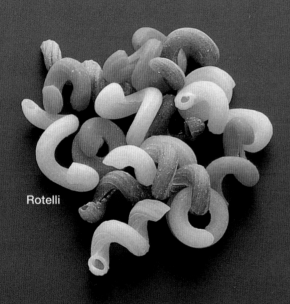
Rotelli

Conchiglie

Fettuccine — tomato, spinach and egg

Egg spaghetti

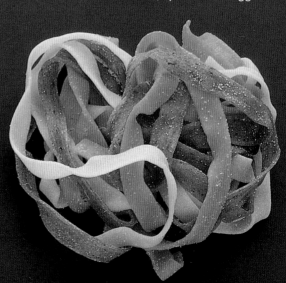

Some dishes rely on a small, subtle coating of the pasta, while others require the pasta to be secondary to a hearty sauce. As a guideline, allow ¼ pound of dried pasta per adult for a main meal and 2 to 3 ounces for a first course or small helping. If cooking fresh and homemade pasta, 5 to 6 ounces is a good main course serving, 3 to 4 ounces for a first course. And what you don't finish can always be eaten the following day!

BEGINNINGS

What better way to start a meal than with a bowl of pasta, delicately sauced or tossed with other flavorful ingredients? Pasta takes so many forms and guises that there is always something appropriate to serve. Many of these recipes make excellent light meals, served with a salad.

SHRIMP AND BASIL SOUP

3 tablespoons olive oil

1½ tablespoons butter

2 cloves garlic

1 small red onion, thinly sliced

2 stalks celery, cut in 1 inch strips

3 small carrots, thinly sliced

1 tablespoon finely chopped fresh parsley

2 tablespoons finely chopped fresh basil

salt and freshly ground black pepper

pinch cayenne pepper

1 pound medium uncooked shrimp, peeled and deveined

½ cup medium dry sherry

4 cups chicken stock

¾ cup (3 ounces) small conchiglie

¼ cup heavy cream

extra fresh basil

1 Heat oil and butter in a large saucepan. Add garlic cloves and onion and sauté gently for 2 to 3 minutes.

2 Add celery and carrots and cook until vegetables are golden; do not brown. Toss in parsley and basil and season to taste. Stir briefly, add shrimp, toss through, then remove garlic cloves.

3 Pour in sherry, increase heat and cook for 2 to 3 minutes. Add chicken stock, bring back to the boil then simmer for 5 minutes.

4 Add conchiglie and simmer until pasta is *al dente*.

5 Stir in cream, adjust seasonings to taste and serve garnished with basil leaves.

SERVES 4

BROCCOLI SOUP

3 tablespoons olive oil

1 large onion, thinly sliced

2 ounces diced prosciutto or unsmoked ham

1 clove garlic, crushed

5 cups chicken stock

⅓ cup stellini or other pastina

½ pound broccoli, tops cut into small florets and the tender stems julienned

salt and freshly ground black pepper

freshly grated Parmesan cheese

1 Heat oil in a large pan and gently sauté onion, prosciutto or unsmoked ham and garlic for 4 to 5 minutes.

2 Pour in stock, bring to the boil and simmer for 10 minutes with the lid three-quarters on.

3 Add stellini and broccoli and cook until pasta is *al dente* and broccoli crisp but tender. Season to taste. Serve at once in warm bowls, passing the Parmesan separately.

SERVES 4

APPLEY HOARE ANTIQUES

PUMPKIN AND LEEK SOUP

**1 small pumpkin, cut in pieces
and seeds removed**

¼ cup butter

2 leeks, white part only, thinly sliced

1 large Spanish onion, chopped

3 to 4 all purpose potatoes, peeled and diced

2 cups milk

2 cups chicken stock

⅓ cup risoni or orzo

salt and white pepper

pinch cayenne pepper

1 cup heavy cream

1 tablespoon finely chopped fresh mint

1 Preheat oven to 375°F.

2 Place pumpkin pieces skin side up and close together in a large baking dish. Pour over ½ cup water and bake for about 1 hour, or until a fork pierces flesh easily.

3 Melt half the butter and gently sauté leeks until softened. Remove and set aside. Add remaining butter and cook onion and potatoes until golden. Stir in milk and simmer for 20 minutes. Don't worry if the milk reduces; just make sure that there is enough liquid to prevent sticking to the pan.

4 When pumpkin is tender and golden, remove from oven, cool, then remove skin and any excessively browned surfaces.

5 In the meantime put chicken stock on to boil, add risoni and cook until barely done. Remove pasta with a slotted spoon and set aside with leeks. Reserve stock.

6 Now blend pumpkin and potato mixture in a food processor or force through a fine sieve. Season with salt, pepper and cayenne to taste.

7 Transfer to a clean saucepan and blend in the hot stock. Add cream, bring to the boil, and then stir in leeks and pasta. If the soup is too thick, thin it with extra stock or water. Adjust seasoning and stir in mint.

SERVES 4 TO 6

Pumpkin and Leek Soup

SPINACH FUSILLI AND ZUCCHINI SALAD

If fresh bocconcini aren't available, don't substitute ordinary mozzarella but choose a fresh, white cheese such as feta or stracchino.

1 cup spinach fusilli

vegetable oil

1 small zucchini, sliced

**4 anchovy fillets, soaked in milk
for 45 minutes**

**2 celery stalks, thinly sliced, plus a few
coarsely chopped tender leaves**

**½ pound cherry tomatoes or small tomatoes
cut into wedges**

½ pound bocconcini, cut into small pieces

**1–2 tablespoons fresh basil leaves,
coarsely chopped**

DRESSING

⅓ cup white wine vinegar

¼ cup olive oil

salt and freshly ground black pepper

1 Cook fusilli in boiling salted water until just *al dente*. Drain, rinse under cold water and drain again. Transfer to a salad bowl and stir with a little vegetable oil to prevent sticking.

2 Sprinkle zucchini with a little salt and drain in a colander for 30 minutes. Rinse, drain, and add to the bowl.

3 Pat dry anchovy fillets, reserve two for decoration and cut the others into small pieces. Add to the salad bowl with celery and leaves, tomatoes, bocconcini and basil.

4 TO PREPARE DRESSING: Combine vinegar, oil, salt and pepper in a jar.

5 Dress the salad, tossing lightly to coat. Garnish with reserved anchovies, cover with plastic wrap and refrigerate for at least 1½ hours before serving.

SERVES 4

≈ **PUMPKIN AND LEEK SOUP**

Baking the pumpkin gives it a special mellow flavor, but if you're pushed for time it can be skinned and boiled with the potatoes.

≈ **BOCCONCINI**

These are little balls of mozzarella with a life of 4 to 5 days. They are eaten for their own sake and usually not used as a melting cheese. Don't substitute matured mozzarella for bocconcini.

This is just as good when made with other cold poultry; the crunch of the sesame seeds and crisp spinach leaves are a good foil for tender poultry meat.

SALAD TRICOLORE

½ pound fresh tomato rotelli or 2 cups dried tomato shapes

1 teaspoon peanut oil

6 to 7 ounces sliced cooked chicken

¼ cup sesame seeds, toasted

1 large bunch curly spinach or swiss chard, rinsed and dried, torn into pieces

1 bunch scallions, thinly sliced, including some green

DRESSING

¼ cup peanut oil

¼ cup olive oil

¼ cup soy sauce

¼ cup rice wine vinegar

2 to 3 tablespoons sugar

salt and freshly ground black pepper

1 Cook pasta in boiling salted water until *al dente*. Drain, rinse under cold water and drain again. Transfer to a salad bowl and stir with a little peanut oil to prevent sticking. Cool.

2 Add chicken and sesame seeds.

3 TO PREPARE DRESSING: In a jar combine all ingredients and shake well.

4 Pour dressing over salad. Cover and chill for at least 2 hours.

5 Toss scallions and spinach through the salad and serve.

SERVES 4 TO 6

These gnocchetti can be served as a tasty side dish with a stew or casserole.

RICOTTA GNOCCHETTI

1 pound ricotta cheese, drained through sieve of cheesecloth

1¼ cups flour

3 tablespoons fine white breadcrumbs

6 ounces grated Parmesan cheese

2 eggs plus 2 egg yolks, beaten together

salt, white pepper and nutmeg

6 tablespoons butter

1 In a bowl combine ricotta, flour, breadcrumbs, half the Parmesan and eggs.

Add a pinch each of the seasonings and blend to form a smooth dough which is dry to the touch. It may be necessary to add a little more flour or a few drops of milk to get the right balance; the moistness of the ricotta will determine this.

2 Knead the dough well, then rest, loosely covered, for 15 minutes. Using your hands, roll the dough into two or three long ropes, ½ inch in diameter. Again rest for 15 minutes before slicing diagonally into ¾ inch lengths.

3 Cook gnocchi in boiling unsalted water for 3 minutes. In the meantime melt butter and cook over a low heat until golden brown. Drain gnocchi and pile on a warm serving plate. Pour over butter and sprinkle with remaining Parmesan before serving.

SERVES 4

TUNA CAVATELLI SALAD

½ pound broccoli, broken into florets

½ pound cauliflower, broken into florets

½ pound cavatelli or other shaped pasta

1 bunch scallions, sliced, including some of the green

4 small tomatoes, cut into wedges

1 clove garlic, thinly sliced

¼ cup finely chopped fresh Italian parsley

½ cup extra virgin olive oil

juice of 1 small lemon

½ teaspoon salt

freshly ground black pepper

One 12¼-ounce can tuna in oil, drained

1 Bring a large pot of water to the boil, add a pinch of salt and the broccoli and cauliflower. Cook for 2 to 3 minutes; they should be still crisp and not soft. Remove with a slotted spoon and rinse under cold water. Shake dry and transfer to a large serving bowl.

2 To the same boiling water add pasta and cook for 15 minutes, or until *al dente*. Rinse under cold water and shake dry.

Transfer to the salad bowl.

3 Add scallions, tomatoes, garlic, parsley, olive oil, lemon juice, salt and pepper to the bowl and mix together lightly.

4 Coarsely flake tuna into bite-sized pieces and toss through the salad. Serve at room temperature.

SERVES 4 AS A LIGHT MEAL

BEAN AND PASTA SALAD

½ pound pennette or other small hollow shape pasta

1½ pounds cooked cannellini beans (or any small white beans)

1 small red onion, thinly sliced

1 thin stalk celery, sliced

2 small tomatoes, cut in wedges

½ cup small black olives

fresh oregano leaves, to garnish

DRESSING

½ cup extra virgin olive oil

2 teaspoons Dijon-style mustard

juice 1 lemon

1 tablespoon finely chopped fresh oregano or parsley

salt and freshly ground black pepper

1 clove garlic, crushed

1 Cook pennette in boiling salted water until *al dente*. Drain, rinse under cold water and drain again. Transfer to a large serving bowl, stir through a little of the oil to prevent sticking together, and cool.

2 Add beans, onion, celery, tomatoes and olives.

3 TO PREPARE DRESSING: Combine all ingredients in a jar and shake well.

4 Pour dressing over salad. Toss thoroughly and taste for salt and pepper. Cover and chill. When ready to serve, toss again lightly and garnish with oregano leaves.

SERVES 4

SAFFRON RISONI SALAD

1½ cups risoni

½ cup olive oil

1 gram pure saffron powder

¾ cup pine nuts

½ cup currants

2 cloves garlic, crushed

juice 1 lemon

¼ teaspoon ground cumin

1 teaspoon ground turmeric

½ teaspoon sugar

salt and freshly ground black pepper

1 small green pepper, thinly sliced in ½ inch lengths

3 tablespoons finely chopped fresh parsley

3 tablespoons finely chopped fresh mint

3 tablespoons finely chopped fresh coriander

coriander leaves, for garnish

1 Cook risoni in boiling salted water for a minute or two less than recommended. Drain, rinse in cold water and drain again. Stir through a little of the olive oil to prevent sticking.

2 Heat oil in a small pan and add saffron, pine nuts and currants. Cook gently until nuts are toasted and saffron gives off its unique aroma. Remove from heat and add garlic, lemon juice, cumin, turmeric, sugar, salt and pepper to taste. Stand for at least 5 minutes.

3 Add sliced pepper, herbs and pine nut mixture to the pasta. Toss before serving, garnished with coriander leaves.

SERVES 4 TO 6 AS A SIDE DISH

≈ **SAFFRON RISONI SALAD**

This delicious spicy 'rice' salad is slightly sweet and so is a perfect accompaniment for broiled or barbecued meals.

When using pasta in a salad, it is important to rinse the cooked pasta with cold water and drain it well. Toss a little oil through the pasta to stop it sticking together.

PASTRAMI, MUSHROOM AND CUCUMBER SALAD

As pastrami is from a lean cut of beef, this dish is low in calories and high in protein and vitamins.

½ **pound lasagnette or wide ribbon pasta, broken into quarters**

½ **pound pastrami, cut in thin strips**

1 **stalk celery, sliced**

2 **small tomatoes, cut in wedges**

1 **seedless cucumber, thinly sliced**

¼ **pound mushrooms, thinly sliced**

¼ **teaspoon finely chopped fresh coriander, for garnish**

DRESSING

¼ **cup olive oil**

3 **tablespoons red wine vinegar**

½ **teaspoon Dijon-style mustard**

salt and freshly ground black pepper

1 **clove garlic, crushed**

¼ **teaspoon Tabasco sauce**

1 Cook lasagnette in boiling salted water until *al dente*; drain and rinse under cold water, then drain again before transferring to a salad bowl.

2 To the salad bowl add pastrami, celery, tomato wedges, cucumber and mushrooms.

3 TO PREPARE DRESSING: Combine ingredients in a jar and shake well to blend.

4 Toss the dressing through the salad and refrigerate, covered, for several hours.

5 Adjust seasoning and sprinkle with coriander before serving.

SERVES 4

TUNA, GREEN BEAN AND ONION SALAD

This salad is equally good served warm or refrigerated overnight and served the next day.

½ **pound stringless green beans, trimmed and cut in 1 inch lengths.**

3 **cups short pasta shapes (fusilli or penne rigate)**

½ **cup olive oil**

½ **pound fresh tuna fillet, sliced in ¼ inch-thick pieces about 2 inches long**

1 **red onion, thinly sliced**

1 **teaspoon balsamic vinegar**

salt and freshly ground black pepper

1 In a large pan of boiling water cook beans for 1 to 2 minutes until tender but still crisp. Remove with a slotted spoon and rinse under cold water. Drain and transfer to a serving bowl.

2 Add salt to boiling water and cook pasta until *al dente*. Drain, rinse under cold water then drain again before adding to beans.

3 Sauté tuna and onion in half the oil until tuna is just cooked through. Add vinegar, turn up heat and quickly cook until dressing has reduced and lightly coats tuna. Transfer tuna and onion to a bowl, leaving behind any bits on the bottom of the pan.

4 Toss beans, pasta, tuna and onion together lightly and mix with remaining oil, and salt and pepper to taste. Cool to room temperature before serving.

SERVES 4

*Tuna, Green Bean and Onion Salad (above) and
Pastrami, Mushroom and Cucumber Salad (below)*

≈ **PASTINA**

Pastina is the generic term for all tiny pasta shapes usually served in soups.

STUFFED PEPPERS AND TOMATOES

The peppers and tomatoes can be eaten hot or cold, and can be served as a first course, a light meal or part of a buffet. They are a good accompaniment to lamb, veal or chicken.

3 large tomatoes, tops sliced off

3 green peppers, tops and seeds removed

4 to 5 tablespoons chicken or vegetable stock

FILLING

3 tablespoons olive oil

1 large onion, chopped

2 cloves garlic, crushed

¼ teaspoon cayenne pepper

salt and freshly ground black pepper

1 tablespoon currants

1 tablespoon pine nuts

1 tablespoon chopped fresh coriander

1 teaspoon chopped fresh parsley

1½ cups cooked risoni or other pastina

4 ounces grated Cheddar or Emmenthaler cheese

1 Preheat oven to 350°F.

2 TO PREPARE FILLING: Heat oil and gently sauté onion and garlic until soft. Add cayenne, salt and pepper to taste, currants, pine nuts, coriander and parsley. Cook until nuts are lightly brown. Transfer to a bowl and combine with pasta and cheese.

3 Scoop pulp from tomatoes, chop finely and add to filling. Mix well.

4 Divide filling between pepper and tomato cases, stuffing lightly. Put peppers into a shallow ovenproof dish, pour a tablespoon of stock over each and bake for 30 minutes.

5 Add tomatoes to the dish and bake for a further 20 minutes, or until tender.

SERVES 6

LUMACHE WITH ARTICHOKES

¼ cup olive oil

1 large onion, roughly chopped

2 cloves garlic, crushed

1 tablespoon dried basil

2 tablespoons chopped fresh parsley

pinch cayenne pepper

1 teaspoon dried oregano

Two 28-ounce cans Italian peeled tomatoes, drained (reserve juice)

¼ teaspoon salt

3 cups (10 ounces) lumache, pipe rigate or other multi-surfaced shape

14 ounces canned artichoke hearts, drained, (reserve juice)

3 tablespoons grated Pecorino cheese

1 Heat oil in a large pot and sauté onion, garlic, basil, parsley, cayenne and oregano for 5 minutes.

2 Roughly chop tomatoes and add to the pot with the salt. Simmer, uncovered, for about 45 minutes, or until reduced and very thick. Add reserved tomato and artichoke juices, stir through and simmer a further 15 minutes.

3 Cook lumache in boiling salted water until *al dente*.

4 Cut each artichoke heart into six and stir into the sauce along with the Pecorino.

5 Drain cooked pasta and add to sauce. Stir well, transfer to warm dishes and serve, passing around extra cheese.

SERVES 4

≈ **PORCINI MUSHROOMS**

The unforgettable taste of fresh porcini mushrooms or cèpes cooked in butter is closely matched by using a combination of the dried variety and fresh plump mushrooms. Choose large ones with lots of white flesh to duplicate the texture and appearance of fresh porcini; flat field mushrooms have too much dark gill section and aren't recommended.

LINGUINE WITH MUSHROOMS

½ ounce dried porcini mushrooms or cèpes

2 tablespoons butter

1 small onion, finely chopped

1 pound very large mushrooms, sliced

1½ tablespoons chopped fresh sage (don't substitute dried)

1½ tablespoons finely chopped fresh parsley

salt and freshly ground black pepper

1 pound fresh linguine or ¾ pound dried

½ cup freshly grated Parmesan cheese

1 Soak porcini mushrooms 30 minutes in hot water to cover. Drain liquid and filter it through cloth or a paper coffee filter to remove grit. Finely slice the mushrooms.

2 Melt half the butter in a frying pan and sauté onion until soft and golden. Add porcini and mushroom liquid and cook until evaporated. Add remaining butter, sliced mushrooms and herbs. Season well and gently simmer, covered, for 15 to 20 minutes.

3 Meanwhile, cook pasta in boiling salted water until *al dente* and drain. Toss with the mushrooms and Parmesan and serve immediately in warmed bowls.

SERVES 4

LIFESTYLE IMPORTS PTY LTD

SPINACH PASTA FRITTATA

½ cup grated Parmesan cheese

5 eggs

½ cup milk

½ cup heavy cream

1½ tablespoons olive oil

1½ tablespoons flour

salt and pepper

½ pound cooked spinach spaghetti or fettuccine

1 tablespoon chopped fresh herbs (parsley, oregano, chives)

1½ tablespoons pine nuts

1 Preheat oven to 350°F.

2 In a bowl mix Parmesan, eggs, milk, cream, oil and flour and season well with salt and pepper. Stir through pasta and herbs.

3 Grease an 8 inch pie pan, and place in it two greased foil strips in the shape of an X. Pour in pasta custard, and sprinkle pine nuts on top. Bake for about 35 minutes, until set and golden.

4 Remove from oven and cool slightly before lifting out, using the foil strips as handles. Serve warm or cold.

SERVES 4 TO 6 AS A LIGHT MEAL WITH SALAD

Linguine with Mushrooms

≈ FRITTATAS

Frittatas are a great way of using precooked pasta. To the basic egg and pasta mixture can be added pieces of ham, salami, mushrooms or cheese. Even leftover sauced pasta can be used, provided that the sauce isn't too runny.

Penne Packets

PENNE PACKETS

½ pound (2½ cups) penne

1½ tablespoons olive oil

2 onions, thinly sliced

4 red peppers, cut into thin strips

5 small tomatoes, cut into thin wedges

1 inch sprig fresh rosemary

salt and freshly ground black pepper

2 small zucchini, julienned

½ cup chicken stock

1 Preheat oven to 375°F.

2 Cook pasta in boiling salted water until barely *al dente* and drain. Stir through a little olive oil to prevent sticking.

3 Heat oil in a large pan and sauté onions and peppers until onions are soft and golden, 10 to 12 minutes; do not brown.

4 Add tomatoes and rosemary, and season to taste. Cook over a low heat, partly covered, for 10 minutes, stirring often.

5 Add zucchini and stock and cook for a further 3 to 4 minutes or until there is about ¼ cup liquid left. Remove rosemary and check seasoning. Stir through penne.

6 Cut four large sheets of aluminum foil (about 12 inches square) and divide the pasta mixture among them. Fold over the foil of each packet and wrap it up tightly so that no steam can escape. Place the bundles in a shallow baking dish and bake for 15 minutes. Serve immediately, being careful of escaping steam when opening the packets.

SERVES 4

≈ PASTA PACKETS

Baking pasta and its sauce in a packet expands the flavors and entraps moisture, keeping the dish succulent. Many pasta-based dishes can be completed this way. Slightly undercook the pasta initially, to leave enough liquid in the sauce for the food to steam. Seal the packets well.

PASTA FLAN

BASE

⅓ pound vermicelli

1½ tablespoons oil

2 eggs, lightly beaten

large pinch nutmeg

2 tablespoons finely grated fresh
Parmesan cheese

salt and freshly ground black pepper

FILLING

½ cup olive oil

1 clove garlic, crushed

One 35-ounce can Italian peeled tomatoes

grated rind ½ large orange

1 tablespoon finely chopped fresh mint

large pinch sugar

¼ pound Fontina cheese or Bel Paese,
cut into small cubes

1 Preheat oven to 375°F.

2 TO PREPARE BASE: Cook vermicelli in
boiling salted water until *al dente*. Drain and
stir through 1 tablespoon olive oil.

3 In a large bowl combine eggs, nutmeg
and Parmesan and season with salt and
pepper. Add vermicelli and stir well to coat
pasta evenly with egg mixture.

4 Grease a 9 inch pie pan and press the
pasta evenly over the bottom and up the
sides to form a shallow rim.

5 Cover the rim loosely with a strip of foil
and bake for 10 minutes, or until set. Don't
remove the foil. Leave oven setting.

6 TO PREPARE FILLING: Heat oil in a frying
pan and gently sauté garlic for 1 minute.
Drain tomatoes, reserving juice, and break
them up with a wooden spoon before adding
to the pan. Cook over a low heat for
5 minutes, stirring occasionally. Season to
taste, and add ¼ cup of reserved tomato juice
and orange rind. Simmer until tomatoes are
pulpy and thick, stirring from time to time.
The mixture should be quite dry with no
excess liquid.

7 Remove from heat and stir in mint and

sugar, then leave to cool slightly. Stir the
cubed cheese into the tomato mixture and
then spoon into the pasta base.

8 Bake until set, about 30 minutes. Cool
slightly before serving.

SERVES 6

PAPPARDELLE WITH SALAMI

1 tablespoon olive oil

1 teaspoon butter

½ small onion, finely chopped

1 clove garlic, crushed

¼ pound salami, thinly sliced and
cut into strips

½ cup dry white wine

One 28-ounce can Italian peeled tomatoes,
drained

1 red pepper, chopped

1 tablespoon golden raisins

1 tablespoon pine nuts

salt and freshly ground black pepper

pinch each ground nutmeg and sugar

½ cup heavy cream

1 pound pappardelle

½ teaspoon chopped fresh mint

1½ tablespoons freshly grated
Parmesan cheese

1 Melt oil and butter in a large saucepan
and gently sauté onion and garlic for
5 minutes. Add salami and then wine,
cooking over a high heat to evaporate.

2 Squeeze seeds and juice from tomatoes,
leaving a very dry pulp. Add this to the pan
along with pepper, raisins and pine nuts.
Season to taste and stir in nutmeg and sugar.
Reduce heat and cook, covered, for 15 to
20 minutes. Add cream and stir through.

3 Meanwhile, cook pappardelle in boiling
salted water until *al dente*, drain. Pour over
sauce, add mint and Parmesan and mix to
coat. Transfer to a warm serving dish, and
serve with extra Parmesan.

SERVES 4

≈ **PASTA PIE BASES**

*Pasta pie bases are an
interesting way of using
precooked ribbon pastas.
Smaller nests for
individual servings are
also attractive: these look
good with chopped parsley
or perhaps poppy seeds
stirred through the pasta
mixture before baking.*

≈ **PAPPARDELLE
WITH SALAMI**

*A sauce with a sweet
intense flavor, this can
be made lighter by
omitting the salami
and keeping the
proportions of the other
ingredients the same.*

ROTELLI WITH TOMATOES AND GREEN OLIVES

9 or 10 ripe tomatoes, peeled, seeded and cut into chunks

¾ cup stoned green olives, sliced

2 cloves crushed garlic

¼ cup finely chopped fresh parsley or basil, or a mixture

salt and freshly ground black pepper

½ cup extra virgin olive oil

2 to 3 drops balsamic vinegar

¾ pound fresh rotelli or 3 cups dried

1 Combine tomatoes, olive, garlic, herbs, salt and pepper in a large serving bowl. Add olive oil and vinegar and toss to coat well. Cover and stand at room temperature for at least 2 hours to allow the flavors to develop.
2 Cook rotelli in boiling salted water until *al dente*; drain. Mix through sauce immediately before serving.

SERVES 4

RIGATONI WITH RICOTTA

½ pound rigatoni or other large hollow tube pasta

vegetable oil

5 tablespoons unsalted butter, melted

freshly grated Parmesan cheese

fresh sage or mint leaves

FILLING

1½ cups ricotta cheese, drained through a sieve or cheesecloth

¾ cup Parmesan cheese, freshly grated

salt and nutmeg

1 Cook rigatoni in boiling salted water until *al dente*; drain, and stir through a little vegetable oil. Cool slightly.
2 Preheat oven to 375°F.
3 TO PREPARE FILLING: Combine ricotta and Parmesan, and add salt and nutmeg to taste. Using a pastry bag with a ½ inch nozzle, stuff each tube well with the ricotta filling.
4 Place stuffed pasta in a greased, shallow ovenproof dish and cover well with the melted butter. Sprinkle with some Parmesan and a few sage leaves. Bake for 15 minutes.
5 Transfer to a warm serving plate, replace the sage leaves with fresh ones and serve.

SERVES 4

SPINACH FETTUCCINE WITH ANCHOVIES

1 pound fresh spinach fettuccine or ¾ pound dried

ANCHOVY SAUCE

3 tablespoons butter

3 tablespoons olive oil

1 small onion, finely chopped

4 to 6 anchovy fillets, finely chopped

¼ pound mushrooms, sliced

freshly ground black pepper

EGG SAUCE

2 egg yolks

1 cup heavy cream

3 tablespoons grated Parmesan cheese

freshly ground black pepper

1 teaspoon chopped chives

1 While preparing sauce, cook fettuccine in boiling salted water until *al dente*.
2 TO PREPARE ANCHOVY SAUCE: Heat butter and oil in a saucepan and gently sauté onion for 5 minutes. Add anchovies and cook briefly until they melt. Add mushrooms and toss to coat. Stir in 2 tablespoons of pasta water. Season with pepper.
3 TO PREPARE EGG SAUCE: Beat together egg yolks, cream and Parmesan.
4 Drain fettuccine and mix with mushrooms. Add egg sauce and chives. Toss until fettuccine is well coated and the sauce is heated through and slightly thickened. Serve with extra Parmesan and black pepper.

SERVES 4

LIFESTYLE IMPORTS PTY LTD

PENNE WITH EGGPLANT AND PECORINO

This dish is rich and strong. You can add other vegetables such as zucchini and olives. For a lighter version using less oil, quickly toss diced eggplant in oil then put under the broiler, turning a couple of times, until browned.

1 medium, firm eggplant, cut in ¾ inch cubes

1 cup olive oil

2 cloves crushed garlic

½ medium-sized green pepper, thinly sliced

One 28-ounce can Italian peeled tomatoes, drained and chopped

salt and freshly ground black pepper

1 pound fresh penne or ¾ pound dried

1½ tablespoons chopped fresh basil or 2 tablespoons fresh parsley

¼ cup Pecorino cheese, grated

1 Place eggplant in a large colander and sprinkle with salt. Leave for at least 30 minutes for the bitter juices to be drawn out by the salt. Squeeze to remove excess liquid and pat dry before cooking.

2 In a large frying pan, heat some of the oil and fry eggplant in batches, adding more oil as needed. As each lot browns, remove from pan, set aside and drain on paper.

3 In the same pan, sauté garlic lightly for 30 seconds. Add pepper and cook for a further minute, then add tomatoes. Season to taste and simmer for 10 minutes. Add eggplant and basil to the sauce and simmer for 2 minutes. Check seasoning then set aside to keep warm.

4 Cook penne in boiling salted water until *al dente*, then drain. Mix with sauce and Pecorino and serve in warmed bowls.

SERVES 4

≈ USING QUALITY INGREDIENTS

As with many recipes where there are few ingredients, the quality of these ingredients makes the difference between a mediocre dish and an exceptional one. Choose the best Parmesan available, and grate it just before use.

PENNE WITH LEEKS, SPINACH AND PIMIENTOS

Mellow but fresh-flavored, this dish can be served as a first course or for a light luncheon followed by cheese and fruit. It is inexpensive, easy and can be made more glamorous simply by adding sliced prosciutto, shrimp or perhaps sautéed fresh tuna.

3 large leeks, trimmed

¾ pound spinach

¼ cup butter

1 small onion, finely chopped

salt and freshly ground black pepper

One 3-inch piece of pimiento cut into thin strips

¾ pound penne rigate

freshly grated Parmesan cheese

1 Slice leeks thinly, using all the whites and most of the greens. Discard spinach stalks and slice leaves thinly.

2 Heat butter in a large pan and gently sauté onion for 4 to 5 minutes. Add leeks and spinach, season well, then cook over a low heat for 10 to 15 minutes. Stir through the pimiento for the last 5 minutes. Adjust seasoning to taste.

3 Cook penne in boiling salted water until *al dente*. Drain and transfer to a warm bowl. Toss with the vegetables and a sprinkling of Parmesan. Serve with extra Parmesan.

SERVES 4

Penne with Leeks, Spinach and Pimientos

AFRICAN HERITAGE GIFT SHOP AND GALLERY

MUSHROOM AND SPINACH LASAGNE

9 dried spinach lasagne sheets or fresh spinach pasta as follows

SPINACH LASAGNE

1 package frozen spinach, thawed

2 eggs

3 cups sifted flour or 2 cups sifted flour and ½ cup semolina

½ teaspoon salt

pinch each white pepper and ground nutmeg

SAUCE

¼ cup butter

1 pound mushrooms, thinly sliced

2 cloves garlic, crushed

¼ teaspoon ground nutmeg

salt and freshly ground black pepper

1 teaspoon fresh lemon juice

¼ cup sifted flour

3½ cups hot milk

RICOTTA MIXTURE

1 pound ricotta cheese

1 small egg, beaten

¼ cup finely chopped fresh parsley

½ cup grated Parmesan cheese

½ pound mozzarella cheese, shredded

1 TO PREPARE SPINACH LASAGNE: Put spinach in a dish towel or cheesecloth and wring it out thoroughly to remove all excess water. Purée in a food processor or blender with 1 egg.

2 Mix flours and seasonings together, then form a well in the center. Break the second egg into the well and beat it with a fork for seven or eight strokes before beginning to incorporate the flour. When the mixture becomes dry, add puréed spinach and work this into the flour. Continue until dough becomes sticky and difficult to work with the fork, then begin to knead by hand using extra flour as needed to form a smooth and elastic ball. Rest dough for at least 20 minutes. This whole step can be done in a food processor if preferred.

3 Divide dough into three or four balls and cover them with a plastic wrap or cloth. Roll each ball into an even, thin sheet, using a pasta machine, or a rolling pin. Rest the sheets before trimming them into workable sizes for cooking.

4 In a large pan of boiling salted water cook the lasagne sheets in batches for 1 to 2 minutes. Remove and drain on dish towels before proceeding. If using dried pasta, cook to desired degree, according to the directions on the package. Drain as above.

5 Preheat oven to 350°F.

6 TO PREPARE SAUCE: Melt butter in a large saucepan and add mushrooms, garlic, nutmeg, salt and pepper. Add lemon juice, then sauté for 2 to 3 minutes. Do not brown. Sprinkle in flour, cook for half a minute, then slowly add hot milk and cook, stirring until thickened into a smooth sauce.

7 TO PREPARE RICOTTA MIXTURE: In a small bowl combine ricotta, egg, half the parsley and most of the Parmesan.

8 Grease a large baking dish or lasagne pan and line it with some of the pasta sheets, bringing them up the sides and extending over the rims; this will form an outer case for the lasagne. Cover with one-third of the ricotta mixture, one-third of the shredded mozzarella and one-third of the mushroom sauce. Place another layer of pasta, just as wide as the dish this time, and continue the sequence of layering, ending with the last of the mushroom sauce on top. Sprinkle with the remaining parsley and Parmesan. Now fold over the pasta flaps and trim, if necessary, so that they form a 1-inch border around the lasagne.

9 Cover the dish loosely with foil and bake for 40 minutes or so. Let stand in a warm spot for 10 minutes before serving.

SERVES 8

≈ **MUSHROOM AND SPINACH LASAGNE**

This lasagne is surprisingly light and makes an excellent luncheon or late supper dish. It can be prepared beforehand and isn't as time-consuming as other lasagne, particularly if you are able to purchase the spinach pasta sheets. It can be made using plain pasta, but the subtle mix of flavors is lessened, along with some of the visual appeal.

MACARONI, CHEESE AND EGG CAKE

1 pound elbow macaroni or ziti

CHEESE SAUCE

2 tablespoons butter

3 tablespoons sifted flour

3 cups hot milk

salt, white pepper and nutmeg

1 to 1½ cups grated Cheddar cheese

2 tablespoons grated Parmesan cheese

1 teaspoon grated onion

2 teaspoons Dijon-style mustard

1½ teaspoons chopped fresh parsley

CRUST

½ cup grated Parmesan cheese

½ cup breadcrumbs

1 egg, beaten

½ pound grated mozzarella cheese

3 sliced hard-boiled eggs

1 Cook macaroni in boiling salted water until *al dente*. Drain and stir through a little vegetable oil to prevent sticking.

2 TO PREPARE CHEESE SAUCE: In a small saucepan melt butter and sprinkle in flour. Cook until smooth. Gradually pour in the hot milk, and cook, stirring, until sauce begins to thicken. Add salt, pepper and nutmeg to taste, onion, Cheddar, Parmesan, mustard and parsley. Continue to cook until thick and smooth. In a bowl combine the pasta with cheese sauce and mix well.

3 Preheat oven to 350°F.

4 TO PREPARE CRUST: Mix Parmesan and breadcrumbs together and sprinkle some in a greased loaf pan. Coat the sides well, and shake out the excess. Pour in egg and swirl around the pan to cover breadcrumb mixture. Discard excess, then shake around a final coating of breadcrumbs and Parmesan.

5 Now layer one-third of the pasta in the bottom of the dish and cover this with one-third of the mozzarella. Place half the boiled egg slices in a single layer on top. Repeat this layering, then on the last level of eggs put the remaining pasta and finally the last of the mozzarella.

6 Bake for 20 to 30 minutes. Allow the cake to cool for 15 minutes, and then run a sharp knife around the edge to loosen it. Carefully turn out onto a warm serving plate and serve in slices.

SERVES 6 TO 8

LINGUINE IN WHITE CLAM SAUCE

One 10-ounce can baby clams

1 cup milk

2 tablespoons olive oil

2 tablespoons butter

1 clove garlic, crushed

1 small onion, finely chopped

¼ pound mushrooms, sliced

½ cup dry white wine

1½ tablespoons finely chopped fresh parsley

1 tablespoon finely chopped fresh basil

1 teaspoon finely chopped fresh oregano or ¼ teaspoon dried

salt and white pepper

1 pound fresh linguine or ¾ pound dried

4 sprigs fresh basil, to garnish

1 Drain clams and soak in milk for 1 to 1½ hours. Drain again, reserving ½ cup of the liquid.

2 Sauté garlic and onion in butter and oil until soft, add mushrooms, sauté briefly, then pour in wine. Cook over medium heat to evaporate slightly, then add the herbs, clams and clam milk. Season well and cook until sauce is somewhat thickened.

3 Meanwhile, cook linguine in boiling salted water until *al dente*. Drain and transfer to a heated serving dish. Pour on the sauce and decorate with sprigs of basil.

SERVES 4

PUMPKIN GNOCCHI

1 small (1½ to 2 pounds) pumpkin, cut in pieces and seeded

½ cup semolina

½ to 1 cup sifted potato flour

salt, white pepper and ground nutmeg

¼ pound unsalted butter

freshly grated Parmesan cheese

1 Preheat oven to 350°F.

2 Place pumpkin in a shallow baking dish, skin side up, pour in 3 tablespoons water and bake until tender.

3 Remove from the oven and cool. Peel off the skin and any burnt surfaces, then mash the flesh or put it through a food mill to yield 2 cups pulp. (It's not recommended to use a blender or food processor, as the resulting purée tends to be watery and lacks body.)

4 Put pumpkin in a large bowl, season and begin to work in the flours. Use all the semolina and as much of the potato flour as gives a soft kneadable dough. Add salt, pepper and nutmeg. Knead lightly until elastic. Cover and rest for 10 minutes.

5 Break off little pieces about ¾ inch long. Roll them quickly between the fingers to obtain a smoother surface, then press them with the thumb against the curved back of a fork or grater to get the traditional gnocchi shape. Dust lightly with potato flour and rest for 10 to 12 minutes.

6 Melt butter in a saucepan and cook it over a medium heat until golden brown. Keep warm.

7 Cook the gnocchi, a few at a time, in boiling salted water. When they rise to the surface remove with a slotted spoon and transfer to warm bowls. Pour the butter over the top, sprinkle on some Parmesan and serve immediately. Extra Parmesan can be served separately.

SERVES 6

≈ PUMPKIN GNOCCHI

Choose a richly-colored pumpkin for good texture and flavor, and work quickly and lightly with the dough to avoid toughness. If you are busy it is possible to boil the pumpkin instead of baking it, but the flavor won't be as intense, nor the texture as firm.

Preparing Pumpkin Gnocchi with brown butter and Parmesan

When frying the chips, don't overcook them. They should look crisp and golden and covered in blisters.

SPINACH CHIPS

2 packages frozen spinach, thawed

1¾ cups semolina

2 eggs

1 teaspoon vegetable oil

1 tablespoon salt

¼ cup grated Parmesan cheese

1 teaspoon freshly ground black pepper

1 teaspoon dried oregano

1 teaspoon onion salt

1 teaspoon garlic salt

vegetable oil for frying

1 Put spinach in a dish towel and wring it thoroughly dry. Mix in a food processor with all the remaining ingredients except frying oil. Blend until a smooth ball of dough forms which slows or stops the machine. If mixing by hand, chop spinach finely first.

2 Knead dough (incorporating some flour if necessary to give a dry but pliable consistency), until dough is smooth and elastic, about 6 minutes. Cover with a damp cloth or plastic wrap and rest for 30 minutes.

3 Divide the ball into four and roll each out very thinly, using a rolling pin or pasta machine. Sprinkle the sheets lightly with flour and let rest 15 minutes. Using a sharp knife or a pastry cutting wheel, cut the sheets into rectangles of about 2 x ¾ inches.

4 Heat oil until a slight haze is visible. Toss in one or two chips to check the temperature, then fry them quickly in batches. It should take 5 to 10 seconds if deep-frying, or 5 to 8 seconds each side if shallow-frying. Remove with a slotted spoon and drain on absorbent paper.

MAKES ABOUT 100

Spinach Chips

RICOTTA AND SALAMI IN WINE PASTA

PASTA

3 cups sifted flour

large pinch salt

large pinch sugar

1 egg, beaten

½ cup dry white wine, or more if needed

FILLING

1 cup ricotta cheese

1 egg

¼ pound smoked mozzarella, finely diced

2½ ounces lean salami, finely diced

1 tablespoon grated Parmesan cheese

¼ teaspoon freshly ground black pepper

2 tablespoons dried breadcrumbs

1½ tablespoons finely chopped fresh mint

beaten egg for sealing

vegetable oil for frying

1 TO PREPARE PASTA: Mix together flour, salt and sugar on a work surface and make a well in the center. Add egg and wine, and begin incorporating dry ingredients with a fork. When a rough dough is formed, begin kneading, adding more flour or wine to make it pliable but dry to the touch. Knead for at least 6 minutes, or until smooth and elastic. Cover with a damp cloth or plastic wrap and rest for 30 minutes. Divide into three and roll each piece out to a very thin sheet. Cover and let rest for 15 minutes before cutting.

2 TO PREPARE FILLING: Combine all ingredients in a bowl and mix well.

3 Cut pasta circles 4 to 5 inches in diameter. Paint the rims with egg, then place a scant tablespoon of filling along the centers. Fold over to form a half-moon shape and press edges together. Cut around the rims with a fluted pastry wheel or seal with the tines of a fork and set aside in a single layer until ready to cook.

4 Heat vegetable oil in a deep-frying pan until a slight haze is visible. Fry pastries, two or three at a time, until golden and crisp on both sides. Remove with a slotted spoon and drain on absorbent paper before serving.

SERVES 3 TO 4

HAM AND MUSHROOM LASAGNE

3 tablespoons olive oil

1 small onion, finely chopped

½ pound mushrooms, sliced

One 28-ounce can Italian peeled tomatoes, drained and finely chopped

¼ cup chopped fresh parsley

dry white wine

salt and freshly ground black pepper

1 pound fresh lasagne sheets or packaged lasagne

toasted fresh breadcrumbs

¾ pound unsmoked ham, cut into strips

½ pound shredded mozzarella

2 hard-boiled eggs, thinly sliced

1 In a large pan heat oil and gently sauté onion until soft. Add mushrooms and sauté briefly, then tomatoes and parsley. Cook, covered, for 40 minutes, adding a little wine if the sauce becomes dry. Season lightly.

2 Preheat oven to 375°F.

3 Cook the lasagne sheets, a few at a time, in boiling salted water until *al dente*. Remove with a large flat slotted spoon or a skimmer and place on dry dish towels to drain.

4 Grease a rectangular baking dish or lasagne pan and coat the sides with breadcrumbs. Discard any surplus.

5 Place a layer of pasta over the bottom and up the sides. Spoon in one-third of the sauce, cover with a layer of ham, then one-third of the mozzarella, and half the egg slices. Cover these with a layer of pasta, half the remaining sauce, and continue the layers until the last is the remaining mozzarella. Fold over the top any pasta from the sides which may be exposed.

6 Bake for 30 minutes. Let sit for a few minutes in a warm spot before serving.

SERVES 4 TO 6

≈ **WINE PASTA**

Pasta made with white wine and a touch of sugar has a flavor reminiscent of yeast dough. If the sugar is left out, the pasta, cut into shapes or ribbons, can be served with a sauce. You can substitute Bruder Basil cheese for the smoked mozzarella in this recipe.

≈ **HAM AND MUSHROOM LASAGNE**

This is a deep-flavored lasagne which can be served as a first course or as the main meal. Made without a white sauce, it makes a less rich dish than other lasagne, and eliminates a time-consuming step. It can be prepared up to 24 hours in advance and kept in the refrigerator until needed.

FAST PASTA

This is what pasta is all about in today's kitchen: a filling meal ready in the time it takes to cook the fettuccine or spaghetti, and one which you have prepared yourself, easily and without fuss. Because the cooking time is brief, the nutritional content of the ingredients is not lost and there's the added bonus that often there is very little washing up.

TOMATO TAGLIERINI WITH FENNEL SAUCE

2 large fennel bulbs

1 pound fresh tomato taglierini or angel hair

¼ cup butter

¼ cup olive oil

1 clove garlic, crushed

½ cup dry white wine

½ pound mushrooms, sliced

salt and white pepper

⅓ cup heavy cream

1 tablespoon finely chopped fresh parsley

3 tablespoons coarsely grated Parmesan cheese

1 Trim fennel bulbs and boil them. Discard any tough outer stalks and slice thinly.

2 Heat butter and oil together in a sauté pan, stir in garlic, and add fennel and white wine. Cook for 1 to 2 minutes, add mushrooms and season with salt and pepper to taste. Stir in cream and parsley and cook for 30 seconds more, and mix in Parmesan.

3 Meanwhile, cook taglierini in boiling salted water until *al dente*. Drain.

4 Mix sauce through pasta and serve with extra grated Parmesan.

SERVES 4

GORGONZOLA AND PISTACHIO FETTUCCINE

The secret of this recipe is to move quickly once the Gorgonzola has been added, to avoid the cheese separating.

½ **pound dried fettuccine or ¾ pound fresh**

2 **tablespoons butter**

3 **tablespoons olive oil**

1 **clove garlic**

2 **tablespoons finely chopped fresh parsley**

¼ **cup shelled pistachio nuts**

½ **cup (¼ pound) Gorgonzola or other creamy blue cheese, e.g. Castello**

3 **tablespoons grated Parmesan cheese**

1 Cook the fettuccine in boiling salted water until *al dente*.

2 Heat butter and oil in a pan, sauté garlic, and add parsley and pistachios. Cook, stirring, for 2 minutes. Remove garlic clove. Add crumbled blue cheese and stir until melted. Mix 2 tablespoons pasta water into the sauce.

3 When pasta is cooked, drain. Stir sauce and Parmesan through fettuccine and serve with extra grated Parmesan.

SERVES 4 AS AN APPETIZER OR LUNCHEON ENTRÉE

TORTELLINI VERDI WITH RICOTTA AND PISTACHIO NUTS

1 **pound spinach tortellini with ricotta filling**

¾ **cup ricotta cheese**

¼ **cup grated Parmesan cheese**

3 **tablespoons heavy cream**

2 **eggs**

salt and white pepper

12 **shelled pistachio nuts, roughly chopped**

1 Begin cooking tortellini.

2 In a blender or food processor combine ricotta, Parmesan and cream and mix until smooth. Transfer to a saucepan and set over a pot of boiling water. Stir occasionally while heating through.

3 Beat eggs with salt and pepper.

4 When tortellini are cooked, drain, stir in the egg mixture then the sauce. Transfer to heated serving dish. Decorate with chopped pistachios and serve with extra grated Parmesan.

SERVES 6 AS AN APPETIZER OR LUNCHEON ENTRÉE

CONCHIGLIE WITH SPINACH AND ALMOND SAUCE

½ **pound small dried conchiglie or ¾ pound fresh**

½ **pound fresh or frozen spinach, cooked and drained**

1½ **tablespoons chopped fresh basil or 1 teaspoon dried**

½ **cup roughly chopped fresh parsley**

1 **cup grated Pecorino cheese**

½ **cup blanched almonds**

2 **cloves garlic, chopped**

¼ **cup softened butter**

¼ **cup extra virgin olive oil**

extra grated Pecorino or grated Pepato

1 Cook conchiglie in boiling salted water until *al dente*.

2 Place all ingredients in a blender or food processor and blend to a smooth paste. Take ¼ cup of the pasta cooking water and blend into the sauce.

3 Drain cooked pasta and stir sauce through it. Serve with extra grated Pecorino, or grated Pepato for added oomph.

SERVES 4 AS A FIRST COURSE OR LIGHT MEAL

≈ **SPINACH AND ALMOND SAUCE**

The beautiful color and good coating quality of this sauce make it very versatile. You can toss in some diced feta cheese, or some crisp bacon pieces or serve the dish in smaller portions as an accompaniment to grilled or poached fish.

Ingredients for Gorgonzola and Pistachio Fettuccine

*Pasta can be precooked
and stored and reheated
successfully if it is made
from durum wheat
semolina. Before freezing
or refrigerating, coat
pasta with a light oil,
cool and stir thoroughly
to prevent sticking. Seal
it well in a bowl before
storing. Before using,
remove from freezer and
let it defrost in the
refrigerator.
Reheat pasta by stirring
it through a hot sauce or
cover it with a damp
cloth and place in a
preheated oven.*

≈ SPAGHETTINI
WITH ZUCCHINI
AND WALNUTS

*This can be varied by
using summer squash
and replacing the
spaghettini with spinach
spaghetti or fettuccine.*

ZUCCHINI WITH SAFFRON SAUCE

1 pound penne or orecchiette

2 tablespoons vegetable oil

2 cloves garlic, crushed

1½ small young zucchini, sliced in ¼ inch rounds

salt, pepper and nutmeg

⅔ cup heavy cream

1 gram saffron

grated Parmesan cheese

1 Cook penne in boiling salted water until *al dente.*

2 Heat oil in a large frying pan and sauté garlic and zucchini until golden brown but still crisp. Add salt, pepper and nutmeg to taste.

3 Meanwhile bring cream and saffron to the boil. Simmer gently until cream is slightly thickened and a mellow saffron color.

4 Reserve a few slices of zucchini for decoration. Drain cooked pasta and add to the zucchini pan with saffron cream. Stir to coat well.

5 Garnish with reserved zucchini. Serve grated Parmesan separately.

SERVES 4 AS A MAIN COURSE

SPAGHETTINI WITH ZUCCHINI AND WALNUTS

1 pound fresh spaghettini or ¾ pound dried

¼ cup olive oil

½ cup small onion, finely chopped

1 clove garlic, crushed

1 cup walnut halves, chopped

4 small zucchini, grated

3 tablespoons finely chopped fresh parsley

1 tablespoon chopped fresh basil or ½ teaspoon dried

salt and freshly ground black pepper

pinch nutmeg

5½ tablespoons butter

3 tablespoons freshly grated Parmesan cheese

1 Begin cooking spaghettini in boiling salted water.

2 Heat oil in a large frying pan and gently sauté onion and garlic until soft. Add walnuts and cook until slightly colored.

3 Add zucchini, parsley and basil and cook, stirring, for 20 seconds. Season to taste with salt, pepper and nutmeg. Add butter and cook until butter is bubbling.

4 When pasta is *al dente*, drain and transfer to heated bowl. Pour over sauce, add Parmesan and toss together before serving.

SERVES 4 AS AN APPETIZER OR LUNCHEON ENTRÉE

FETTUCCINE WITH RICOTTA AND DILL SAUCE

1 pound fresh whole wheat fettuccine or ¾ pound dried

1 clove garlic, crushed

2½ cups (1¼ pounds) ricotta cheese

1½ cups milk

1½ teaspoons salt

pinch each white pepper and cayenne pepper

pinch red pepper flakes

½ red pepper, chopped

2 tablespoons chopped fresh dill

1 Cook fettuccine in boiling salted water until *al dente.*

2 In blender or food processor, blend garlic, ricotta, milk, salt, peppers and red pepper flakes to form a smooth sauce. Transfer to a bowl. Stir through pepper and dill.

3 When pasta is *al dente*, mix 1 to 2 tablespoons cooking water through the sauce, then drain pasta. Add sauce to pasta and mix to coat before serving.

SERVES 4

VERMICELLI WITH WALNUT SAUCE

This dish goes very well before a main meal of fish or poultry. The rich, crunchy sauce keeps well in the refrigerator for up to 4 days, and it is also good served as a dip with crudités.

¾ pound fresh vermicelli or ½ pound dried

1¼ cups fresh walnut halves

1 large bunch fresh parsley, roughly chopped (to make 2 cups)

¼ cup fresh or dried breadcrumbs

6 tablespoons butter, softened

½ cup good olive oil

¼ cup heavy cream

salt and white pepper

1 Begin cooking pasta in boiling salted water.

2 Place walnuts, parsley and breadcrumbs in a food processor or blender and chop until finely ground. Add butter and oil and blend again to form a thick green paste.

3 Finally, add cream and season to taste with salt and pepper. Blend to combine.

4 Drain cooked pasta and transfer to a warm serving dish. Mix with sauce and serve immediately. It is not usual to serve cheese with this dish.

SERVES 4 AS AN APPETIZER OR LUNCHEON ENTRÉE

Walnut Sauce

VILLA ITALIANA

GNOCCHI WITH FONTINA SAUCE

½ pound Fontina cheese, grated or finely chopped

½ cup heavy cream

5½ tablespoons butter

¼ cup grated Parmesan

1 pound gnocchi dumplings

few leaves of fresh sage for garnishing

1 Place Fontina, cream, butter and Parmesan in a double boiler or a bowl in a saucepan of simmering water. Heat, stirring occasionally, until the cheeses have melted and the sauce is smooth and hot.

2 In the meantime start boiling water for the gnocchi, and when the sauce is about halfway done, put in the gnocchi. Drain cooked gnocchi and coat with a little vegetable oil.

3 Pour sauce over gnocchi, garnish with sage leaves, and serve immediately.

SERVES 4

BAKED PASTA WITH ZUCCHINI AND MOZZARELLA

¾ pound shaped pasta (fusilli, orecchiette or conchiglie)

¼ cup olive oil

5 small zucchini, cut into ½ inch rounds

salt and freshly ground black pepper

One 28-ounce can Italian peeled tomatoes, drained, seeded and chopped

8 to 10 black olives, sliced

3 tablespoons freshly grated Parmesan cheese

1 teaspoon fresh rosemary sprigs

½ pound mozzarella cheese, cut into ½ inch cubes

1 Cook pasta in boiling salted water.

2 In a large frying pan, heat oil and sauté zucchini until lightly browned, about 5 minutes. Season with salt and pepper and transfer to an oiled shallow casserole dish.

3 Preheat oven to 350°F.

4 When pasta is almost cooked, drain and add to zucchini. Add tomatoes, olives Parmesan, rosemary and one-third of the mozzarella. Sprinkle with a little more salt and pepper if desired and gently mix together.

5 Cover with remaining mozzarella and bake until cheese is melted and the top slightly browned, about 15 minutes.

SERVES 4

TAGLIERINI WITH SUN DRIED TOMATOES AND SNOW PEAS

¾ pound fresh taglierini or ½ pound dried

⅓ cup extra virgin olive oil

3 or 4 cloves garlic, crushed

1 tablespoon finely chopped fresh mint

1 tablespoon finely chopped fresh parsley

12 to 15 small snow peas sliced diagonally into thirds

10 to 12 sun dried tomatoes, rinsed, drained and sliced thinly

juice ½ lemon

salt and freshly ground black pepper

1 Begin cooking taglierini in boiling salted water.

2 Heat oil and very gently sauté garlic and herbs for 1 to 2 minutes. Add snow peas and toss for 1 minute, and then stir in tomatoes. Add lemon juice, and season to taste with salt and pepper.

3 Drain cooked taglierini and stir it into the pan with the vegetables. Serve immediately.

SERVES 4

≈ GNOCCHI WITH FONTINA SAUCE

Fresh sage and cheese have an affinity that gives a subtle flavor hard to duplicate with dried sage. So if fresh sage is not available, try adding a different flavor, such as julienned red pepper or thin strips of sun dried tomatoes stirred through the sauce just before serving.

≈ TAGLIERINI WITH SUN DRIED TOMATOES AND SNOW PEAS

There is no substitute for sun dried tomatoes. If unavailable, leave them out of the recipe.

Gnocchi with Fontina Sauce

TUNA, OLIVE AND CAPER SAUCE

One 12¼-ounce can tuna in water

3½ tablespoons butter

3 tablespoons sifted flour

1 cup hot milk

salt and white pepper

1 tablespoon chopped fresh parsley

1 tablespoon chopped chives

juice ½ lemon

12 black olives, sliced

1 tablespoon small capers

4 to 5 drops Tabasco sauce

1 Drain tuna and reserve liquid. Melt butter in a large saucepan and add flour. Cook, stirring, until smooth and golden. Add hot milk and reserved liquid and gradually stir to a thick, smooth sauce.

2 Season to taste with salt and pepper and stir in parsley and chives. Add lemon juice, olives, capers and Tabasco sauce; stir well. Break up tuna into smaller chunks and add to sauce; cook to heat through.

SERVES 4

≈ BUYING AND USING SCALLOPS

Scallops should be firm, with creamy white meat and a pleasant smell. Scallop meat can be stored in the refrigerator for up to 3 days in an airtight container.

TAGLIATELLE WITH SCALLOPS AND SMOKED SALMON

3 tablespoons unsalted butter

1 clove garlic, crushed

1½ tablespoons grated onion

16 small scallops soaked in milk
for 30 minutes

1 pound fresh tagliatelle or ¾ pound dried

⅔ cup dry white wine

1 tablespoon finely chopped fresh parsley

salt and white pepper

⅔ cup heavy cream

¼ pound smoked salmon, julienned

1 Heat butter and gently sauté garlic clove and onion for 1 to 2 minutes. Increase heat, add drained scallops and quickly stir fry until opaque.

2 Put tagliatelle on to cook in boiling salted water.

3 Add wine and parsley to scallops and over a high heat reduce juices by half. Season to taste, then stir in cream. Lower the heat and cook to slightly thicken the cream.

4 Drain tagliatelle when *al dente* and transfer to a warm serving dish. Pour over sauce, add smoked salmon and toss quickly before serving.

**SERVES 4 AS AN APPETIZER
OR LUNCHEON ENTRÉE**

ROTELLI WITH SPINACH AND ANCHOVIES

¾ pound fresh rotelli or ½ pound dried

4 tablespoons butter

3 cloves garlic, crushed

8 anchovy fillets, finely chopped

1 pound spinach, chopped, cooked
and drained

One 28-ounce can Italian peeled tomatoes,
drained

¼ cup toasted pine nuts

1 Cook rotelli in boiling salted water until *al dente*.

2 Gently sauté garlic in butter for 30 seconds, then add anchovies and cook for a moment or two more. Add spinach and stir to evaporate any remaining moisture; the mixture should be quite dry at this stage.

3 Squeeze tomatoes to remove excess juice, and add pulp to pan.

4 Drain cooked pasta, leaving a little cooking water, and combine with spinach mixture before serving. It is not recommended to serve cheese with this dish.

**SERVES 4 AS AN APPETIZER
OR LUNCHEON ENTRÉE**

SEAFOOD WITH FRESH TAGLIATELLE

Very easy and very quick, this dish requires fresh pasta (preferably made from durum wheat semolina) to enable fast cooking in the final step. The result is a deliciously fresh combination of flavors.

⅓ cup olive oil

2 cloves garlic, crushed

1 pound lobster tails cut into pieces with shells left on

1 pound medium shrimp, shelled and deveined with tails left on

¾ pound white fish fillets, cut into pieces

2 large tomatoes, peeled, seeded and chopped

1 small jar pimientos, chopped

1 teaspoon paprika

1 gram saffron

salt

4 cups light fish stock

2 pounds fresh tagliatelle

1 In a large frying pan heat oil and add garlic. Sauté briefly and add seafood. Cook, stirring, until well coated with garlic and oil and shellfish begins to turn pink.

2 Add tomatoes, pimientos, paprika, saffron, and salt to taste. Pour in stock and bring to the boil. Add tagliatelle, stir in and simmer until *al dente*, 1 to 3 minutes. If it looks as though there will be excess juice left, increase the heat for the last half minute.

3 The dish is ready when the pasta is cooked. Take the pan to the table and serve immediately.

SERVES 6 TO 8

Seafood with Fresh Tagliatelle

≈ PREPARING SHRIMP

Cut off the head and remove the shell. The tail doesn't have to be removed. Use a sharp knife to slit the center and back and pull the vein out.

≈ PENNE WITH
SHRIMP AND BACON

*This combination appears
to break all the rules —
bacon with shellfish, cheese
with seafood and hot with
cold — but with delicious
results. Cooking time is
minimal and here is one
instance where frozen peas
are preferable to fresh, as
their texture when thawed
allows for a good
saturation of the bacon
drippings.*

≈ COOKING
WITH LIVER

*Calf's liver or lamb's
liver can be used but
either way cook only
when ready to eat; liver
reheated becomes dry,
tough and sharply
flavored.*

TORTELLINI WITH SAUSAGE

1 pound meat tortellini

1½ tablespoons butter

½ green pepper, sliced

**3 good quality hard Italian sausages,
preferably spicy, cut in ¾ inch pieces**

¾ cup ricotta cheese

½ cup Pecorino cheese, grated

salt and freshly ground black pepper

1 Cook tortellini in boiling salted water.

2 Melt butter and sauté pepper and sausages
until sausages are browned and cooked
through. Keep warm.

3 In a bowl combine ricotta and Pecorino,
a little salt and generous grindings of black
pepper. Just before serving, beat through
1 to 2 tablespoons boiling pasta water.

4 Drain tortellini and transfer to a warm
serving dish. Add ricotta and sausage
mixtures and blend to distribute evenly.

SERVES 4

PAPPARDELLE WITH LIVER AND BACON

1 pound fresh pappardelle or ¾ pound dried

3½ tablespoons butter

1 clove garlic

1 small onion, thinly sliced

¼ pound bacon, sliced into short strips

**2 teaspoons chopped fresh sage or
½ teaspoon dried**

¾ pound liver, cleaned and sliced into strips

¼ cup dry vermouth

1 tablespoon tomato purée or juice

salt and freshly ground black pepper

1 Begin cooking pappardelle in boiling
salted water.

2 Melt butter in a large frying pan and
gently sauté garlic clove and onion until
soft; do not brown.

3 Add bacon and sauté until crisp, and then

add sage and liver. Increase heat slightly and
sauté until liver is just brown.

4 Remove garlic clove and add vermouth
and tomato purée; reduce. Season to taste,
and add a little stock or extra tomato purée
if too dry.

5 When the pasta is *al dente*, drain, and mix
in the pan with the liver before serving.

**SERVES 4 AS AN APPETIZER
OR LIGHT MAIN MEAL**

PENNE WITH SHRIMP AND BACON

1 pound penne rigate

**¼ pound bacon, cut into
narrow strips**

¼ cup frozen peas, thawed

**½ pound medium shrimp, peeled
and trimmed**

2 tablespoons butter

½ cup ricotta cheese

**salt and freshly ground
black pepper**

**1½ tablespoons grated
Parmesan cheese**

1 Cook penne in boiling salted water.

2 In a large frying pan heat bacon until fat
begins to melt. Stir in thawed peas and sauté
for 1 to 2 minutes before adding shrimp.
Cook until just done. Remove from heat and
stir in butter until melted.

3 In a bowl combine ricotta, salt, pepper
and Parmesan. Just before serving, add 1 or
2 tablespoons boiling pasta water and whisk
through. Drain penne when *al dente* and mix
in ricotta. Add bacon, shrimp and peas and
toss together before serving.

SERVES 4

LASAGNETTE WITH CHICKEN LIVERS

½ pound small green beans, trimmed

1 pound lasagnette

2 tablespoons walnut oil

2 tablespoons butter

¾ pound chicken livers, trimmed and cut in half

¼ pound small mushrooms, sliced

1 teaspoon balsamic vinegar or 1 tablespoon sherry vinegar

salt and white pepper

½ cup chicken stock

1 tablespoon chopped Italian parsley

5 to 6 walnut halves, roughly chopped (optional)

1 In a large pot of boiling water, blanch beans for 1 minute. Remove with a slotted spoon and rinse under cold water; drain. Add lasagnette to the boiling water with a pinch of salt and cook until *al dente*; drain.

2 Meanwhile, heat oil and butter in a large frying pan and add livers. Sauté quickly until browned on the outside but pink and juicy inside. Toss mushrooms through, then add vinegar. Increase heat slightly and reduce juices.

3 Season to taste, then pour in stock and quickly reduce by half. Toss in beans and lasagnette and stir in parsley. Serve on warm plates decorated with walnuts.

SERVES 4

SMOKED TURKEY AND CAVATELLI SALAD

⅓ pound cavatelli or orechiette

3 tablespoons olive oil

½ pound smoked turkey, sliced into 1 to 1½ inch pieces

½ cup mushrooms, sliced

1½ tablespoons chopped fresh chives

freshly ground black pepper

1 teaspoon balsamic vinegar

1 tablespoon extra virgin olive oil

1 avocado, quartered and sliced

¼ pound smoked cheese (e.g. mozzarella or Bruder Basil) cut into ½ inch cubes

1 Cook pasta in boiling salted water until *al dente*. Drain, rinse in cold water, then stir in a little oil to prevent sticking.

2 Heat olive oil in a large frying pan and sauté turkey pieces, mushrooms and chives until turkey is lightly browned. Season well with black pepper. Add vinegar and extra virgin olive oil and cook, stirring, until the juices have reduced and thickened. Season again. Add pasta and toss well; cook for 10 to 15 seconds.

3 Remove pan from the heat and toss in avocado slices and cheese. Stir through well to distribute the heat; then let the dish rest for 2 to 3 minutes before serving. Serve warm, or cool completely and serve at room temperature.

SERVES 4 AS AN APPETIZER

OR LUNCHEON ENTRÉE

Tomato Fettuccine with Scallops

TOMATO FETTUCCINE WITH SCALLOPS

¼ pound unsalted butter

3 cloves garlic, crushed

¼ pound mushrooms, sliced

2 tablespoons fresh lemon juice

½ pound fresh scallops

4 very small zucchini, cut into 1 inch straws

3 tablespoons finely chopped parsley

salt and freshly ground black pepper

pinch cayenne pepper

1 pound fresh tomato fettuccine

3 tablespoons chopped parsley, to garnish

1 In a large frying pan melt half the butter and sauté garlic for 1 minute; do not brown.

2 Add mushrooms and lemon juice and toss well. Add scallops with zucchini and parsley. Cover and steam gently, shaking frequently for 1 to 2 minutes. Add remaining butter; when melted, blend and season to taste. Add cayenne.

3 Meanwhile, cook pasta in boiling salted water until *al dente* and drain. Stir in sauce, garnish with parsley and serve.

SERVES 4

LASAGNETTE WITH MUSHROOMS AND CHICKEN

¼ cup milk

**½ teaspoon dried tarragon or
1 tablespoon fresh**

1 pound lasagnette

1½ tablespoons butter

2 cloves garlic

½ pound sliced chicken breast

¼ pound mushrooms, sliced

**1 tablespoon porcini mushrooms,
soaked 30 minutes in hot water
to cover (optional)**

salt, pepper and nutmeg

2 cups cream

few sprigs fresh tarragon, for garnish

1 Put milk and tarragon in a small saucepan and bring to the boil. Remove from heat and let steep. If using porcini mushrooms, drain liquid and filter it through cloth or paper coffee filter to remove grit. Reserve liquid and chop mushrooms.

2 Begin cooking lasagnette in boiling salted water.

3 In a frying pan melt butter and gently sauté garlic, chicken and mushrooms until chicken is golden and cooked through. Discard garlic cloves and add chopped porcini (if used), and the strained soaking liquid. Add salt, pepper and nutmeg to taste and stir for 10 seconds or so before pouring in cream and tarragon milk. Stir well, bring to the boil and simmer until sauce thickens.

4 Drain pasta when it is *al dente* and transfer to a warm serving plate. Taste sauce for seasonings, then add to pasta and toss through. Serve decorated with tarragon.

SERVES 4

*Lasagnette with
Mushrooms and Chicken*

SAUCES

The secret's in the sauce, and there's no denying that it's hard to beat a delicious bowl of pasta served with your favourite sauce. The range available means that there is always a sauce that is right for the occasion. As some sauces are traditionally served as part of particular dishes, we have included whole meals here, as well as individual sauces.

PESTO GENOVESE

Pesto is traditionally served with trenette, but can go on any ribbon pasta and is very good on cheese-filled ravioli. It can be used in soups, on salads and steamed vegetables, and is perfect for drizzling over baked tomatoes. It is essential to use fresh young basil, and the sauce is at its best when a quality extra virgin olive oil is used. For variations, try Pepato cheese instead of plain Pecorino to give a more piquant flavor, or substitute a proportion of tender spinach leaves for some of the basil.

pinch salt (optional)
1 bunch fresh basil leaves, loosely chopped
2 cloves garlic
⅓ cup olive oil
¼ cup pine nuts, lightly toasted
½ cup freshly grated Parmesan cheese
½ cup freshly grated Pecorino cheese
¼ teaspoon toasted breadcrumbs (if using food processor)

1 USING A PESTLE AND MORTAR: Add a pinch of salt to the basil, garlic, 1 tablespoon oil and a few pine nuts and begin crushing. Continue adding pine nuts and oil until you have a smooth texture. Blend in cheeses and stir well.

2 USING A FOOD PROCESSOR OR BLENDER: Add basil, garlic, breadcrumbs, pine nuts and cheeses. Chop thoroughly, and continue to blend as you gradually pour in olive oil, until a mayonnaise-like texture is obtained.

SERVES 4

≈ PESTO

Pesto can be kept successfully for 5 to 7 days in the refrigerator if the surface is covered with a thin layer of olive oil, and can be frozen if you omit the cheeses and stir them through after defrosting. However, aficionados maintain that it should be made just before needed, and that storing the sauce changes the composition of the ingredients.

Ingredients for Pesto Genovese

Some ingredients for Sauce of Four Cheeses

SAUCE OF FOUR CHEESES

1½ tablespoons butter

1 teaspoon flour

¾ cup hot milk

3 ounces Fontina cheese, shredded

3 ounces Provolone cheese, grated

3 ounces Emmenthaler cheese, grated

3 ounces mozzarella cheese, shredded

freshly grated Parmesan cheese, to serve

1 Heat butter in a saucepan and when it starts to foam, stir in flour. Cook for half a minute and then whisk in milk. Continue cooking over a gentle heat, stirring, until thickened and smooth. Remove from heat and beat in all the cheeses except Parmesan.

2 Place the saucepan over a pot of boiling water and heat until sauce is smooth, stirring often. Don't boil once the cheeses have been added or the sauce will separate. Serve over hot pasta with extra grated Parmesan.

SERVES 4 AS AN APPETIZER OR LUNCHEON ENTRÉE

SORREL AND SPINACH SAUCE

½ pound fresh sorrel, leaves only

½ pound spinach, leaves only

salt

3½ tablespoons butter

3 tablespoons olive oil

1½ tablespoons finely chopped fresh parsley

1½ tablespoons finely chopped fresh basil

freshly ground black pepper

pinch ground nutmeg

½ cup heavy cream

1 Rinse sorrel and spinach under cold water and shake off excess. Put in a large pot with

a pinch of salt but no extra water and cook gently, covered, until limp and tender. Drain, press out excess water, and chop finely.

2 Melt butter and oil in a large frying pan and add sorrel, spinach and herbs. Season with a little salt, lots of black pepper and a good pinch of nutmeg. Cook gently for 5 minutes, then add cream and simmer for 5 minutes more.

SERVES 4 TO 6

CHEESE AND NUT SAUCE

This is a good coating sauce which can be made in advance, but its success depends on using fresh walnuts (preferably just from the shell), and fresh basil. It can be served on vegetables too, and is particularly fine on green beans.

½ cup shelled walnuts

¼ cup pine nuts, toasted

1 teaspoon toasted fresh breadcrumbs

3 tablespoons fresh basil leaves

salt and freshly ground black pepper

1 clove garlic, crushed

3 tablespoons olive oil

1½ tablespoons freshly grated Parmesan cheese

¼ cup ricotta cheese

1 In a food processor or blender, place nuts, breadcrumbs, basil, salt and pepper. Blend until they form a coarse paste, then add garlic and oil.

2 Transfer to a bowl and stir through Parmesan and ricotta. Continue to mix until the sauce is smooth. Taste for salt and pepper, and add a little more Parmesan if a sharper flavor is preferred.

3 Serve over any hot pasta. Before mixing, add one tablespoon of the pasta cooking water to thin the sauce slightly and increase the temperature.

SERVES 4 AS AN APPETIZER

OR LUNCHEON ENTRÉE

'PICCHI-PACCHI'

½ cup olive oil

1 large onion, thinly sliced

1 clove garlic, crushed

4 anchovy fillets, drained and soaked in milk for 45 minutes

One 14-ounce can Italian peeled tomatoes, drained and chopped

1 sprig fresh basil

salt and freshly ground black pepper

1 In a large pan heat oil and sauté onion and garlic until soft.

2 Add drained anchovies and cook for 1 to 2 minutes, breaking them up with the spoon as you stir.

3 Add tomatoes and basil, season lightly and simmer, covered, for 20 minutes or so until smooth and thick. Adjust seasoning. No grated cheese is served with this sauce.

SERVES 4

BAKED TOMATO SAUCE

One 28-ounce can Italian peeled tomatoes, drained and mashed

2 cloves crushed garlic

1 onion, finely chopped

1 tablespoon minced fresh basil or 1 teaspoon dried

¼ cup olive oil

red pepper flakes

½ cup fresh breadcrumbs mixed with ⅓ cup grated Parmesan cheese

1 Preheat oven to 400°F.

2 Combine tomatoes, garlic, onion, basil and oil in a baking dish and sprinkle with a few red pepper flakes. Sprinkle breadcrumb mixture over the top and bake uncovered for 30 minutes.

3 Don't break up the crust until the sauce is mixed through the pasta; large crunchy bits should remain.

SERVES 4

≈ **'PICCHI-PACCHI'**

'Picchi-pacchi' is a rich, full-flavored sauce which can be served on most types of pasta, but coming from Sicily it more often than not appears on spaghetti. There is a version which includes fried eggplant, and another which has black olives thrown in for the last 5 minutes of cooking.

≈ **BAKED TOMATO SAUCE**

This sauce has a unique flavor that stove-top tomato sauces can't match. It can be easily adapted by adding olives, salami, sautéed vegetables, shrimp or just about anything and it complements all types of pasta.

SAUCE OF LEEKS, GRUYÈRE AND CREAM

1½ tablespoons unsalted butter

1 clove garlic

1 large leek, thinly sliced, white only

3 tablespoons sifted flour

salt, white pepper and nutmeg

¾ cup hot milk

2 cups heavy cream

¼ pound Gruyère cheese, grated

1 Melt butter in a saucepan and add garlic and leek. Over a low heat gently cook leek, stirring often, until golden and softened, about 8 minutes.

2 Stir in the flour and season to taste with salt, pepper and nutmeg. Cook until flour changes color slightly.

3 Remove garlic clove and then gradually add the milk, stirring all the time. When sauce is smooth and thick, pour in cream. Bring back to the boil, lower the heat and cook for 5 minutes.

4 Add Gruyère and cook, stirring, until cheese has melted. Remove from heat and cool slightly before serving. This sauce keeps well refrigerated for up to four days.

SERVES 4

≈ RED PESTO

Red Pesto is a good coating sauce with an intriguing tang to it. Served over pasta shapes or ribbons, it makes a piquant first course well suited to precede a main meal of grilled or baked tuna steak. It keeps well in the refrigerator for up to 4 days.

RED PESTO

3 to 4 anchovy fillets, soaked in milk for 45 minutes

large pinch salt

1 clove garlic, crushed

⅓ cup toasted pine nuts

1½ tablespoons dried breadcrumbs

1 cup red pimientos, roughly chopped

⅓ cup canned tomatoes, drained and seeded

1 tablespoon capers

1 teaspoon dried oregano

1½ tablespoons chopped fresh parsley

3 to 4 tablespoons red wine vinegar

½ cup olive oil

1 In a blender or food processor blend drained anchovies, salt, garlic, pine nuts and breadcrumbs. Add pimiento and tomatoes and process until a red paste forms.

2 Add capers, oregano and parsley and blend. Add vinegar. Gradually add oil and mix until sauce is the consistency of pesto.

3 Stir through hot pasta. Before mixing, add one tablespoon of the pasta cooking water to thin the sauce slightly.

SERVES 4

SPAGHETTI ALLA PUTTANESCA

⅓ cup olive oil

2 cloves garlic, crushed

pinch red pepper flakes

6 anchovy fillets, soaked 30 minutes in milk, then drained

One 28-ounce can peeled tomatoes, drained and pulped, reserve juice

¾ cup sliced black olives

1½ tablespoons capers

1 sprig fresh oregano or ¼ teaspoon dried

1 pound fresh spaghetti or ¾ pound dried

1 tablespoon chopped fresh parsley

1 Heat oil in a large frying pan, sauté garlic and red pepper flakes, then add anchovies and stir until melted.

2 Add tomatoes, olives, capers and oregano and cook over medium heat for 10 minutes. If sauce becomes too dry, add some reserved tomato juice.

3 Cook spaghetti in boiling salted water until *al dente*. Drain, and transfer to a warm serving dish. Pour sauce over the top and sprinkle with parsley.

SERVES 4

MARINARA SAUCE

A marinara sauce is basically tomatoes and garlic reduced to a rich sauce. You can have an artichoke marinara, one made with olives or, of course, a seafood marinara.

¼ cup olive oil

2 cloves garlic, crushed

1 small onion, chopped

¼ cup chopped fresh parsley or half parsley and half fresh basil

6 large tomatoes, peeled, seeded and chopped or one 35-ounce can Italian peeled tomatoes, drained and pulped

pinch sugar

salt and freshly ground black pepper

1 Sauté garlic and onion in oil until soft and golden, about 10 minutes; do not brown.

2 Add herbs, tomatoes, sugar, salt and pepper. Simmer, stirring occasionally, until sauce is thick and mellow, about 30 minutes.

SERVES 4

PISTACHIO MAYONNAISE

3 egg yolks

1 cup extra virgin olive oil

salt and freshly ground black pepper

juice ½ lemon

1½ tablespoons finely chopped fresh basil

3 tablespoons finely chopped fresh parsley

3 tablespoons ground pistachio nuts

1 Whisk egg yolks in a bowl. Continue to whisk and pour in oil in a very slow trickle, until it has all been absorbed. Still whisking, add salt, pepper and lemon juice to taste. Stir through basil, parsley and nuts to give a smooth, very thick sauce.

2 If the mayonnaise appears to be curdling, continue its preparation to the finish. Beat another egg yolk in a clean bowl and gradually whisk in the curdled sauce. The mayonnaise will keep, covered and chilled, for up to 24 hours.

SERVES 4 TO 6

Pistachio Mayonnaise

≋ PISTACHIO MAYONNAISE

This is delicious served over hot fresh herb fettuccine or with cold shellfish and sugar-snap peas in a pasta salad. It is less successful if made with a food processor or blender. Perhaps it's the moisture in the fresh herbs being crushed that disrupts the balance of things; whatever the reason, the sauce is more likely to curdle if made with a machine and the texture and color also suffer.

BUCATINI ALL'AMATRICIANA

This sauce from the town of Amatrice depends on a light tomato flavor and the crispness of the bacon. It used to be milder, but as tastes changed, a hotter sauce has gradually evolved. For variations add 1 or 2 tablespoons of chopped parsley and/or garlic, both of which nicely complement the basic ingredients.

1 pound bucatini

2 tablespoons olive oil

1 small onion, finely chopped

1 dried red pepper or flakes to taste

One 28-ounce can Italian peeled tomatoes, drained and chopped

¼ pound thickly sliced pancetta or bacon, diced

3 tablespoons freshly grated Parmesan cheese

1 Begin cooking bucatini in boiling water.

2 Heat half the oil in a frying pan and sauté onion and red pepper, until softened. Add tomatoes and simmer for about 7 minutes; this sauce is not thick.

3 Meanwhile, fry pancetta in the remaining oil until crisp. Keep warm.

4 When the pasta is *al dente*, drain and place in a warm bowl. Toss through Parmesan, sauce and lastly pancetta.

SERVES 4

≈ **FETTUCCINE WITH PEAS AND HAM IN EGG SAUCE**

This is also good with some sliced mushrooms fried with the leeks.

FETTUCCINE WITH PEAS AND HAM IN EGG SAUCE

¾ pound fresh or frozen young peas

1 cup chicken stock

¼ pound unsalted butter

2 leeks, white part only, thinly sliced

¼ pound sliced ham, julienned

1 pound fresh fettuccine or ¾ pound dried

2 medium-sized eggs

¾ cup freshly grated Parmesan cheese

salt and freshly ground black pepper

1 Cook peas in chicken stock until tender. Set aside with 3 tablespoons cooking liquid.

2 Melt butter and gently fry leeks until soft and golden. Stir in peas, stock and ham. Cover and keep warm.

3 Begin cooking fettuccine in boiling salted water. While it is cooking, beat eggs with half the Parmesan and season with salt and pepper.

4 When the pasta is just cooked, drain it (not too well; some water can remain) and toss immediately with egg mixture. Quickly stir in ham and pea sauce. Pour into warmed serving dish. Serve with remaining Parmesan and extra pepper.

SERVES 4 AS A LIGHT MEAL

SPAGHETTINI WITH LEMON, HAM AND CREAM

¾ pound dried spaghettini or 1 pound fresh

6 tablespoons unsalted butter

⅓ pound sliced ham, cut into thin strips

1 cup heavy cream

1½ tablespoons finely chopped fresh parsley

grated rind 1 lemon

salt and freshly ground black pepper

2 tablespoons grated Parmesan cheese

1 Begin cooking spaghettini in boiling salted water.

2 Melt butter in a large deep frying pan and add ham. Cook for 30 seconds before adding the cream, parsley and lemon rind. Season with salt and pepper and cook for a further 1 to 2 minutes until thick and smooth.

3 When pasta is *al dente*, drain and add it to the pan. Toss quickly with the grated cheese to coat well and heat through. Serve with additional grated Parmesan.

SERVES 4

Bucatini All'Amatriciana

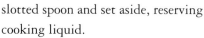

LIFESTYLE IMPORTS PTY LTD

≈ **PAGLIA E FIENO WITH BACON, PEAS AND MUSHROOMS**

If dried porcini can't be found, look for cèpes. If reducing the amount of parsley, reduce the amount of cream also, so sauce retains the right consistency.

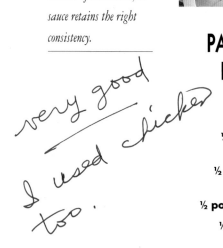

very good
I used chicken too.

PAGLIA E FIENO WITH BACON, PEAS AND MUSHROOMS

½ **pound fresh plain fettuccine or ⅓ pound dried**

½ **pound fresh spinach fettuccine or ⅓ pound dried**

½ **pound shelled peas, fresh or frozen**

½ **pound bacon, cut into strips, rinds reserved**

1 **tablespoon dried porcini mushrooms, soaked 30 minutes in hot water to just cover (optional)**

½ **pound mushrooms, sliced**

1 **clove garlic, crushed**

1 **teaspoon freshly ground black pepper**

1 **bunch fresh parsley, finely chopped**

2¼ **cups cream**

grated Parmesan, to serve

1 Cook peas until tender in a large saucepan of boiling salted water; remove with a slotted spoon and set aside, reserving cooking liquid.

2 Fry bacon rinds in a large pot until crisp and fat is extracted. Discard rinds and fry bacon in the fat until crisp.

3 Drain porcinis and filter liquid through cloth or a paper coffee filter to remove grit. Chop finely and add to the pot with the soaking liquid and fresh mushrooms. Stir in garlic and pepper and cook briefly. Toss in parsley and cook for 30 seconds.

4 Add cream and cook, stirring, until the sauce comes to the boil. Boil until thickened and reduced, 5 to 8 minutes.

5 Begin cooking fettuccine in the water used for the peas. When *al dente*, drain and transfer to a warm serving dish. Toss with the sauce, and serve with freshly grated Parmesan.

SERVES 4

PENNE ALL'ARRABBIATA

2 tablespoons dried porcini mushrooms
(optional)

3 tablespoons olive oil

1 onion, finely chopped

2 cloves garlic, crushed

¼ pound pancetta or unsmoked bacon,
cut into strips

One 28-ounce can Italian peeled tomatoes,
drained and chopped

¼ teaspoon red pepper flakes

1 pound penne

2 tablespoons grated Pecorino cheese

3½ tablespoons butter, cut into slivers
and kept cold

1 If using porcinis, soak 30 minutes in hot water to cover, drain and cut into thin strips. (Juice should be filtered through paper and may be reserved or frozen for another use.)

2 Heat oil in a large saucepan and sauté onion and garlic gently for 5 minutes. Add pancetta and sauté for a further 5 minutes.

3 Add porcini, tomatoes and red pepper flakes and simmer over moderate heat until thickened and rich, 20 to 30 minutes. Taste for seasoning and add more pepper flakes if you like. If the sauce appears to be drying out, stir in 1 to 2 tablespoons pasta cooking water.

4 Begin cooking pasta in boiling salted water and when it is just *al dente*, drain.

5 Add penne and Pecorino to sauce, mix in butter until it melts, and serve.

SERVES 4

≈ COMBINING SAUCE AND PASTA

A step practised by a lot of Italian cooks is to unite the sauce with the pasta straight after cooking. This keeps everything hot and results in a quick and even distribution of flavors; you can save a little of the sauce for decoration, if desired. When using a cold sauce with hot pasta, for example Pesto, mix a couple of tablespoons of the pasta water through the sauce to warm, and help it coat more readily.

SAUCE FROM BOLOGNA

4 tablespoons butter

1 small onion, finely chopped

1 stalk celery, finely chopped

1 small carrot, finely chopped

2 ounces pancetta or bacon, finely chopped

1 bay leaf

¾ pound ground beef

1½ teaspoons sifted flour

½ cup dry red wine

½ cup beef stock

½ ounce dried porcini mushrooms (optional)

salt and freshly ground black pepper

pinch nutmeg or cloves

½ cup milk

2 tablespoons cream

1 minced chicken liver

1 Soak porcini mushrooms (if using) 30 minutes in hot water to cover. Drain liquid and filter it through cloth or a paper coffee filter to remove grit. Finely chop the mushrooms.

2 In a large pot melt butter and gently sauté onion, celery, carrot, pancetta and bay leaf for 8 to 10 minutes.

3 Add ground beef, increase the heat slightly and cook until golden brown. Sprinkle in flour, stir through and cook for 30 seconds before adding wine. Stir over a high heat until most of the wine has evaporated.

4 Add porcinis and their liquid, and taste for salt before seasoning. Add nutmeg and half the stock and simmer over a low heat, covered for 1½ hours.

5 Stir from time to time and add remaining stock. When two-thirds through add milk and adjust seasonings. Just before serving stir in cream and chicken liver and cook, uncovered, for a final minute or two.

SERVES 4

≈ SAUCE FROM BOLOGNA

The true Bolognese sauce bears little resemblance to that which is found outside Italy; it's not even served with spaghetti, but tagliatelle, another creation of Bologna. Like the city, the sauce is mellow yet sophisticated. Its flavor comes from long gentle cooking and the milk softens and sweetens it. No garlic is necessary and tomatoes aren't used, although some like to add a tablespoon or two of tomato paste for extra richness and color.

≈ SAUCE CONSISTENCY

Pasta sauces should have a good thick consistency, so if cream is called for, make it heavy. However, if using light cream or half and half, increase the cooking time slightly.

FINE FARE

A delicious, filling meal can be made with all types of pasta. Serve long pasta (fettuccine, taglierini, spaghetti or linguine) with a good thick sauce based on oil, tomato, cream or soft melting cheeses. Twisted or hollow pasta (fusilli, cavatelli or rotelli) is best with chunky sauces. Long fine strands (vermicelli or angel's hair) are delicious with clinging sauces made of butter and cheese, raw tomato, or an egg base, and wide flat noodles like pappardelle or lasagnette go with gutsy meaty sauces.

≈ COOKING
FOR MANY

If you are cooking for a crowd, precook pasta in batches, then oil it lightly and keep it warm in the oven covered with a damp cloth.

FARFALLE WITH SMOKED SALMON AND MASCARPONE

1 pound farfalle

2 leeks, white part only, thinly sliced

3½ tablespoons butter

½ deep red pepper, julienned

1 pound (2 cups) mascarpone or Devon (double thick) cream

½ pound smoked salmon, cut into thin strips

salt and white pepper

chopped fennel tops (optional)

1 Cook farfalle in boiling salted water until *al dente*.

2 Cook leeks gently in melted butter for a few minutes, being careful not to brown them. Reserve a few pieces of pepper for decoration, and add the rest to the leeks. Cook for a further 30 seconds.

3 Add mascarpone, or cream, and bring to the boil. Stir in most of the smoked salmon and cook just long enough to heat through. Taste for salt and add a pinch if needed. Add a pinch of pepper. Toss in the fennel tops (if using).

4 Mix with the drained pasta and decorate with reserved pepper and salmon.

SERVES 4

APPLEY HOARE ANTIQUES

≈ **PROSCIUTTO**

This is unsmoked, uncooked, salted, air-cured ham. It should be succulent and sweet, not too salty.

PASTA AND BEAN SOUP

Pasta and beans is common to many regions where they each have their special recipes. In Venice they like their pasta and beans flavored with a touch of cinnamon and the bone from a Parma ham; a subtle but unforgettable flavor sometimes enhanced with Parmesan cheese.

½ pound dried kidney beans, soaked in water overnight

1 prosciutto or ham bone

1 onion, chopped

pinch cinnamon

cayenne pepper

1 tablespoon olive oil

2 cups chicken stock

¼ pound tagliatelle, plain or spinach, broken into 1 to 2 inch pieces

Pasta and Bean Soup

1 Drain and rinse beans, cover with cold water in a saucepan and bring to the boil. Stir, then boil for 15 minutes.

2 Drain beans and transfer to a large pot with ham bone, onion, cinnamon, pinch of cayenne, olive oil and stock. Add cold water to cover. Cover pot well and simmer until beans are cooked and have begun to thicken the stock. Remove bone and cut off any meat from it. Flake this and return to the pot; discard bone.

3 Taste for seasoning; salt may be needed, depending on the bone used. Bring the soup back to the boil, add pasta and cook until it is *al dente*. Let rest off-heat for 1 to 2 minutes before serving.

SERVES 5 TO 6

BAKED MUSHROOM AND RICOTTA PACKETS

PASTA
2 cups sifted flour

salt

2 eggs plus 2 yolks, beaten together

1½ tablespoons melted butter

1½ cups milk

extra melted butter

FILLING
3 tablespoons butter

1 pound mushrooms, sliced

¼ teaspoon each salt, freshly ground black pepper and nutmeg

3 tablespoons toasted fresh breadcrumbs

¼ cup finely chopped fresh parsley

1 pound ricotta cheese

¼ pound mascarpone

1½ tablespoons grated Parmesan cheese

1 egg plus 1 yolk, beaten together

TOPPING
½ cup grated Parmesan cheese

5 tablespoons melted butter

1 TO PREPARE PASTA: Sift flour and a pinch of salt into a bowl. Add beaten eggs and butter and stir to combine. Gradually mix in milk until a thick batter is obtained. Continue to beat a further 7 or 8 minutes to get a smooth consistency. Rest for at least 5 minutes.

2 Heat some of the extra butter in a small frying pan, and then pour in enough batter to thinly cover the bottom. Lightly cook on each side, until golden. Remove from the pan and repeat with remaining batter, buttering the pan as necessary. There should be 6 to 8 cooked crepes, depending on the size of your pan. Trim each one neatly into squares and set aside.

3 TO PREPARE FILLING: Sauté mushrooms over high heat until golden but still firm. Season with salt, pepper and nutmeg and stir

in breadcrumbs and parsley. Transfer the mixture to a bowl and mix with ricotta, mascarpone, Parmesan and eggs. Combine well.

4 Preheat oven to 400°F.

5 Place equal amounts of filling in the center of each cooked pasta sheet, then fold the corners of each over, in the manner of an envelope, to form a package. Arrange in a buttered shallow ovenproof dish. Sprinkle top with Parmesan and melted butter and bake until golden, about 15 minutes.

SERVES 4

CHICKEN, LEEK AND CHICKPEA SOUP

4 cups chicken stock

1 cup tiny pasta shapes (ditalini, tiny shells)

1½ tablespoons butter

1 leek, white part only, sliced

1 clove garlic

½ cup roasted chickpeas (available in specialty food stores)

1½ tablespoons sifted flour

3 tablespoons finely chopped Italian parsley

salt and freshly ground black pepper

pinch cayenne pepper

1 cup chopped cooked chicken meat

1 Put chicken stock in a saucepan and bring to the boil. Add pasta and cook until barely done. Remove pasta, but keep stock just boiling.

2 Meanwhile, sauté leek and garlic in butter until golden, not brown. Add chickpeas, toss for a minute and then sprinkle with the flour. Cook for 10 seconds or so, then gradually blend in boiling stock.

3 Add parsley, salt and cayenne and a good half dozen grinds of the pepper mill. Add pasta and chicken meat and bring back to the boil before serving.

SERVES 4

≈ **HEALTHY PASTA PACKETS**

This method of baking filled pasta packets is great for the diet conscious, as it does away with the need for the sauce that conventional cannelloni require.
Be careful not to overbake, or the pasta will toughen and dry, and don't use too much butter when cooking the crepes.

≈ **CHICKEN, LEEK AND CHICKPEA SOUP**

The subtle flavor of this soup can be made even more interesting by using fresh coriander instead of parsley, and adding a pinch of red pepper with the leek.

The herb pasta, minus its filling, can be used for a stunning appetizer or light meal. Simply cut it into squares and serve with a light sauce such as pistachio mayonnaise or pesto. Flat squares of pasta, known as quadrucci, can be any size from small pieces used in soups, to larger elegant sheets of 3 to 4 inches square served with a sauce.

SPICY RICOTTA AGNOLOTTI IN HERB LEAF PASTA

PASTA

3 cups sifted flour

pinch salt

3 eggs, lightly beaten

nicely shaped leaves of any flat-leaved herb (Italian parsley, chervil or coriander), reserve some for decoration

1 egg, beaten

FILLING

1 pound ricotta

3 tablespoons grated Parmesan cheese

pinch grated nutmeg

pinch cayenne

salt

approximately ½ cup fresh breadcrumbs

TO FINISH

½ cup light olive oil

4 cloves garlic

freshly grated Parmesan cheese

fresh herbs

1 TO PREPARE PASTA: Mix flour and salt in a processor for a second or two. Add whole eggs and continue to process until a smooth ball forms. Incorporate more flour or a little water, if necessary. Cover dough with a damp cloth or plastic and rest for 30 minutes.

2 Divide dough into four and, working one quarter at a time, roll out until a thickness is reached which is twice that of your final pasta. A pasta machine is perfect for this. Do not flour the surface before the next step.

3 Take some herb leaves and discard thick or fleshy stems, then separate into attractive sections of about ½ inch each. Place 1 to 2 inches apart over half the pasta sheet. Fold the plain half over this and roll out. It may be necessary to roll the pasta at this thickness several times to fully press the herb, which will take on a delicate stretched appearance.

4 Cover each sheet with plastic wrap.

5 Using a 3 to 4 inch biscuit cutter, cut circles over the herbs on the pasta sheets, keeping the finished circles covered as you work.

6 TO PREPARE FILLING: Mix first five ingredients together, then add breadcrumbs until a light but manageable texture is reached.

7 Lay out half a dozen circles, paint their edges with egg and place some filling across the center. Fold each one over to encase filling, press edges together and trim with a fluted pastry wheel or tines of a fork. Set aside, uncovered, until all are done.

8 TO FINISH: Heat oil in a large pan or wok and gently sauté garlic over a low heat. Discard garlic and keep oil warm.

9 Cook agnolotti in boiling salted water until *al dente*. Drain, then transfer to the pan with the olive oil and toss to coat.

10 Serve immediately with a sprinkling of herb leaves and Parmesan.

SERVES 4

TAGLIATELLE WITH ZUCCHINI AND BASIL

6 small zucchini, halved then quartered

5 tablespoons unsalted butter

½ cup vegetable oil

1½ tablespoons sifted flour

1 cup milk

1 pound fresh tagliatelle
or ¾ pound dried

½ cup heavy cream

¾ cup fresh basil, finely chopped

1 Put zucchini slices in a colander, sprinkle with a little salt and leave to drain for 30 minutes; pat dry with cloth.

2 Heat a little butter and oil in a large pan and sauté zucchini until brown but still crisp. Remove from heat and set aside.

3 Melt rest of oil and butter in a saucepan. Add flour and cook, stirring until the paste is smooth and slightly colored. Gradually whisk in milk and simmer sauce until thickened and smooth.

4 Begin cooking tagliatelle in boiling salted water. Add cream to the white sauce and return to a boil. When thickened, remove from heat and stir in zucchini and basil. When the pasta is *al dente*, drain and transfer to a warm serving dish. Pour the sauce over it and serve immediately.

SERVES 4

≈ **TAGLIATELLE WITH ZUCCHINI AND BASIL**

This has a delicate balance of flavors which should not be missed when young basil is available. It is an excellent dish to precede a main course of veal kidneys or liver.

Tagliatelle with Zucchini and Basil

VILLA ITALIANA

Carrot-flavored pasta has a fresh, slightly nutty flavor which can be served a number of different ways. Here, with a cream sauce, it is rich and sweet.

Fresh Carrot Pasta

FRESH CARROT PASTA WITH CREAM AND MINT

PASTA

1 cup diced carrots

2 eggs

2 teaspoons vegetable oil

1¼ cups semolina

1¾ cups sifted flour

1 teaspoon salt

pinch nutmeg

pinch white pepper

SAUCE

1 cup julienned carrots

3 tablespoons butter

1 tablespoon finely chopped fresh mint

1¼ cups cream

salt and white pepper

1 TO PREPARE PASTA: Purée carrots finely in a food processor or blender. If using a food processor, add the rest of the ingredients and process to form a dough.

2 To mix by hand, place flours and seasonings in a pile on a work surface and make a well in the center. Add eggs, oil and carrot purée and begin working into the dry ingredients with a fork until a roughly formed dough results. Now take the dough and begin kneading by hand, incorporating extra flour if needed, to form a smooth, elastic ball. This will take 8 to 10 minutes. Cover with a damp cloth or plastic wrap and rest for 30 minutes.

3 Divide the dough into three and, working one-third at a time, roll into very thin sheets using a rolling pin or pasta machine. Trim to rectangles approximately 8 inches long; then cover and rest for 15 minutes.

4 If cutting by hand, roll up each rectangle along its length and slice in ¼ inch widths which unroll to become taglierini. If using a pasta machine, cut to desired width. Dust the ribbons lightly with flour and let rest, uncovered, to dry slightly.

5 TO PREPARE SAUCE: Blanch carrots in boiling water until tender but-crisp. In a saucepan melt butter and gently sauté mint for 30 seconds. Add cream and simmer, uncovered, to thicken. Season the sauce lightly and add the carrots. Put pasta on to cook in boiling salted water. Drain pasta when it is *al dente*, stir through a little vegetable oil and then transfer to warm plates. Pour on the sauce and serve at once.

SERVES 5 TO 6

SEAFOOD PASTA SALAD

⅓ pound fresh fettuccine or 1 cup dried
(include some tomato flavored if possible),
cut or broken into short lengths

⅓ pound calamari cut in rings

⅓ pound clam meat, or 1 small can, drained

¾ cup milk

2 tablespoons olive oil

½ pound cooked shrimp, cut in half if large

1 very small red onion, thinly sliced

1 small red pepper, sliced

1 stalk celery, sliced

1 to 2 tablespoons chopped fresh dill

12 cherry tomatoes, yellow or red

DRESSING

¾ cup olive oil

2 cloves garlic, crushed

juice 1 lemon

2 tablespoons white wine vinegar

salt and freshly ground black pepper

1 Cook pasta in boiling salted water until
al dente. Drain, rinse under cold water and
drain again. Transfer to a large serving bowl
and stir through a little of the olive oil.
2 Soak calamari rings and clams in milk for
at least 30 minutes, drain, and then sauté
them gently in remaining olive oil until the
calamari is opaque and tender. Transfer to
the salad bowl.
3 Add shrimp, onion, pepper and celery and
toss lightly.
4 TO PREPARE DRESSING: Combine
ingredients thoroughly and pour over salad.
Add half the dill and toss lightly to coat.
Chill for 1 hour or more. When ready
to serve, decorate with remaining dill
and tomatoes.

SERVES 3 TO 4

PASTA SALAD WITH CHICKEN, SHRIMP AND MELON

1¼ cups elbow macaroni or other
medium-sized pasta shape

vegetable oil

¾ pound chicken fillets

salt and freshly ground black pepper

2 tablespoons butter

1 honeydew melon

¾ pound small shrimp, cooked, peeled
and deveined

2 to 3 celery stalks, finely sliced

DRESSING

3 tablespoons mayonnaise

¼ cup plain yoghurt

2 tablespoons heavy cream

¼ teaspoon Tabasco sauce, or to taste

1 teaspoon chopped fresh dill, plus a
few sprigs to garnish

1 teaspoon gin (optional)

sugar

1 Cook pasta in boiling salted water until
just *al dente*. Drain, rinse under cold water
and drain again. Transfer to a salad bowl and
stir through a little vegetable oil.
2 Season chicken breasts and cook them in
butter until golden. Cool, then slice into
strips and add to the pasta.
3 Cut out the flesh of the honeydew using a
melon baller, and add these to the salad bowl
along with the shrimp and celery.
4 TO PREPARE DRESSING: Mix together
mayonnaise, yoghurt, cream, Tabasco, dill
and gin and season to taste with salt, pepper
and sugar. Pour over salad and toss gently.
Cover with plastic wrap and chill for 1 hour
or more before serving.

SERVES 4 TO 6

≈ **HONEYDEW MELON**
*Cantaloupe can be
substituted for honeydew
melon in this recipe.*

TAGLIATELLE AND BROAD BEANS

½ pound shelled, fresh young fava or lima beans

1½ tablespoons olive oil

2 cloves garlic

¼ pound pancetta or bacon, roughly diced

1 pound fresh tagliatelle or ¾ pound dried

1 stalk celery, sliced

1 teaspoon Dijon-style mustard

1 tablespoon finely chopped fresh parsley

salt and freshly ground black pepper

juice ½ lemon

1½ tablespoons extra virgin olive oil

½ pound Parmigiano Reggiano, cut into ½ inch cubes (best quality Parmesan cheese)

1 Cook beans in boiling water until *al dente*, about 2 minutes, depending on their freshness. Drain, rinse under cold water and drain again. When cool enough to handle, skin the beans then set aside.

2 Heat oil in a frying pan and sauté garlic cloves and pancetta until the latter is crisp and light brown.

3 Begin cooking tagliatelle in boiling salted water.

4 To the frying pan add celery, mustard, parsley, salt and pepper. Stir and cook for 1 minute. Remove garlic cloves from the pan and add beans, lemon juice and extra virgin olive oil. Stir quickly to heat.

5 When pasta is *al dente* drain and add to the pan along with the Parmesan. Toss briefly before transferring to individual plates.

6 Serve with freshly grated Parmesan cheese and freshly ground pepper.

SERVES 4 AS AN APPETIZER

OR LIGHT MEAL

SMOKED TROUT WITH FUSILLI

1 pound fresh fusilli or ⅔ pound dried

3 tablespoons olive oil

2 tablespoons finely chopped leek

One 14-ounce can Italian peeled tomatoes, drained and pulped

large pinch nutmeg

¼ teaspoon ground black pepper

¾ cup heavy cream

salt

½ cup brandy

½ pound smoked trout fillets, sliced into 1-inch pieces

LEMON PARMESAN CRUMBS

3 tablespoons grated Parmesan cheese

1 tablespoon dried breadcrumbs

1 tablespoon finely chopped fresh parsley

rind of 1 lemon, grated

1 Begin cooking fusilli in boiling salted water.

2 In a frying pan, heat oil and cook leek gently until soft but not browned, about 3 minutes. Chop tomato pulp roughly and add to the leeks. Cover and cook over a low heat for 3 to 4 minutes. Stir in nutmeg and black pepper. Add cream.

3 Cover and cook gently for another minute or two. Taste for salt, as some smoked trout can be salty.

4 Drain pasta when it is three-quarters done and add to the sauce with the brandy. Increase heat and cook, stirring often, until the sauce is slightly thickened. Add trout and stir until heated through, 20 seconds or so.

5 TO PREPARE LEMON PARMESAN CRUMBS: Combine ingredients and mix well. Serve separately.

SERVES 4

GREEN SALAD PRIMAVERA

½ pound fresh spinach fusilli, rotelli or other shape, or ⅓ pound dried

½ pound shelled fresh peas

¼ pound very young green beans, trimmed and halved

½ pound fresh asparagus, cut into 1½ inch pieces

½ pound broccoli florets

2 small zucchini, sliced diagonally

few sprigs fresh tarragon, for garnish

DRESSING

¼ cup olive oil

2 tablespoons fresh lemon juice

1 teaspoon Dijon-style mustard

1 tablespoon finely chopped fresh tarragon or ½ teaspoon dried, crumbled and steeped in 1 teaspoon olive oil for 45 minutes

salt and freshly ground black pepper

1 Cook pasta in boiling salted water until just *al dente*. Drain, rinse under cold water and drain again. Transfer to a bowl and stir through a little olive oil to prevent it sticking together.

2 Separately blanch all the vegetables until tender but still crisp; drain, rinse under very cold water and drain again. Add to pasta.

3 TO PREPARE DRESSING: Combine all ingredients. Pour over the vegetables and toss lightly to coat. Decorate with tarragon sprigs. Can be served immediately, but is best if refrigerated for 1 to 2 hours first.

SERVES 5 TO 6 AS A LIGHT MEAL

Green Salad Primavera

RICOTTA AND BASIL LASAGNE

**1 pound fresh lasagne sheets or
¾ pound dried**

4 tablespoons butter

2 tablespoons sifted flour

salt and white pepper

pinch nutmeg

2 cups warm milk

**1½ tablespoons finely chopped
fresh basil**

½ cup ricotta cheese

½ cup grated Parmesan cheese

1½ tablespoons extra chopped fresh basil

*Ricotta and Basil
Lasagne*

1 Cook the lasagne sheets in boiling salted water, a few at a time, until *al dente*. Remove carefully and drain between dish towels.

2 Melt butter in a saucepan and stir in flour. Add a little salt, pepper and nutmeg and cook over a gentle heat until flour begins to change color. Slowly whisk in warm milk until sauce is smooth and thickened. Remove from heat and stir in 1 tablespoon basil, the ricotta and half the Parmesan. Check seasonings.

3 Preheat oven to 400°F.

4 In a greased baking dish, or lasagne pan, place a sheet of pasta, followed by a thin layer of ricotta mixture. Sprinkle this with some Parmesan and extra basil. Continue to layer in this order, finishing with the last of the sauce and Parmesan.

5 Bake for just 20 minutes and serve hot.

**SERVES 4 TO 5 AS AN APPETIZER
OR LUNCHEON ENTRÉE**

TUNA AND SPINACH ROTOLO

PASTA

3 cups sifted flour

large pinch salt

3 eggs, beaten

FILLING

2 pounds fresh spinach

**One 12½-ounce can tuna in oil,
drained and flaked**

6 to 8 anchovy fillets, finely chopped

½ cup grated Parmesan cheese

1 cup fine white fresh breadcrumbs

3 eggs, beaten

salt and freshly ground black pepper

1 TO PREPARE PASTA: Pile flour and salt onto a work surface and make a well in the center. Add eggs and begin to incorporate them into the flour, using a fork, until a rough dough is formed. Use your hands and

ACCOUTREMENT COOK SHOPS

begin kneading, adding a little flour or water if necessary as you go. Continue until a smooth, elastic dough is obtained, about 6 minutes. Cover with a damp cloth or plastic wrap and rest for 30 minutes.

2 TO PREPARE FILLING: Remove stems from spinach leaves and discard. Rinse leaves under cold water and shake off the excess. Place in a large pot with a good pinch of salt and cook, covered, over a low heat until wilted and tender. Drain and cool slightly. Squeeze out any excess water and chop spinach finely. Put in a large bowl and add tuna, anchovies, Parmesan, breadcrumbs, eggs, a little salt and lots of black pepper. Mix thoroughly.

3 TO ASSEMBLE: Roll out the dough to a large, even rectangle ⅛ inch thick. Place on a lightly floured cloth. Spread the filling over the dough, leaving a good inch around the edges. Roll up the dough, jelly roll fashion, using the cloth to help lift and roll smoothly. Firmly wrap the roll in a thin layer of cheesecloth and tie off the ends securely with string. Place in a long narrow pan, like a fish-poacher, cover with lightly salted cold water and bring to the boil. Lower the heat and simmer for 15 to 20 minutes. Allow the rotolo to cool slightly in the cooking water before removing. Carefully take off the cloth and cut into slices for serving.

SERVES 6

≈ **STUFFED PASTA ROLLS**

Stuffed pasta rolls can be presented in several different ways. The slices can be arranged down a long, shallow serving dish and topped with a hot light sauce such as fresh tomato; or they can be placed in a buttered ovenproof dish, sprinkled with Parmesan and butter and placed under a hot broiler for 5 minutes. For a milder flavor and slightly crisper texture, pour melted butter over the uncut roll and place in a very hot oven for 4 to 5 minutes. Rotolos make an eye-catching buffet dish and are ideal served as an elegant appetizer or for a light luncheon.

PENNE AND FRESH TUNA WITH RAISIN AND ALMOND SAUCE

2 tablespoons butter
1½ pounds fresh tuna steaks, cut into strips
¾ pound penne
2 egg yolks, beaten

SAUCE
6 tablespoons butter
3 tablespoons sifted flour
¼ teaspoon nutmeg
salt and white pepper
1 cup white wine
2 tablespoons currants
⅓ cup raisins
¼ cup blanched almonds, slivered
1 tablespoon fresh lemon juice
1 teaspoon sugar

1 Melt butter in a large pan and gently sauté tuna until cooked through. Transfer to a plate and keep warm.

2 TO PREPARE SAUCE: Cook flour in butter, stirring, until the roux is smooth and golden. Add nutmeg, salt and pepper to taste and cook briefly. Gradually pour in wine, stirring constantly.

3 When the sauce is smooth stir in currants, raisins, almonds, lemon juice and sugar, bring to the boil and simmer over a low heat for 20 minutes.

4 Cook penne in boiling salted water until *al dente*. Drain, stir through a little oil to prevent sticking, and transfer to warm plates.

5 Whisk a little of the hot sauce through the egg yolks, then, off the heat, whisk this mixture back into the sauce; keep warm.

6 Top pasta with the pieces of tuna, pour over sauce and serve.

SERVES 4

≈ **PENNE AND FRESH TUNA WITH RAISIN AND ALMOND SAUCE**

Here the rich, gamey flavor of tuna is nicely balanced by dried fruit and nuts. To vary, use a white-fleshed fish such as cod or haddock, and omit the currants and raisins. Double the amount of almonds and toast them in the butter before making the roux.

*A mild but rich sauce,
this can be varied by
omitting the cream and
stirring the cooked pasta
through the sauce in the
pan before serving. It
works as well using plain
fettuccine and tossing
through slices of tomatoes
at the end.*

SCALLOPS AND ROASTED PEPPERS WITH TAGLIERINI

*If time is pressing, this sauce can be made quickly
by substituting canned or bottled pimientos for
the roasted pepper.*

**1 pound fresh taglierini or ¾ pound
dried thin flat pasta**

1 red pepper

1 green pepper

1 pound fresh scallops

salt and freshly ground black pepper

sifted flour

3 tablespoons olive oil

1 clove garlic

1 tablespoon chopped fresh parsley

juice ½ lemon

2 leeks, white part only, thinly sliced

1 cup chicken stock

**3 tablespoons toasted fresh breadcrumbs
mixed with grated rind 1 lemon**

1 Roast peppers under a hot broiler until
charred and blistered on all sides. Remove
from heat and place in a plastic bag, tied off,
to sweat. Remove when cool, peel and seed,
then slice into strips.

2 Season scallops and coat them in flour.
Heat oil, add garlic and quickly sauté
scallops until just brown. Remove from the
pan and sprinkle with parsley and lemon
juice. Remove garlic clove.

3 Add leeks to the pan and sauté until soft.
Pour in stock, increase the heat slightly and
reduce by half. Add scallops and pepper to
the leeks and heat through.

4 Cook pasta in boiling salted water until *al
dente*. Drain and add to the sauce. Stir to coat
and adjust seasoning if necessary. Serve at
once, sprinkled with the lemon
breadcrumbs.

SERVES 4

SEAFOOD AGNOLOTTI WITH CORIANDER AND ZUCCHINI

PASTA

4 cups sifted flour

large pinch salt

4 eggs

FILLING

**½ pound white fish fillets (cod, ocean
perch, or haddock), poached, boned
and minced**

**1½ tablespoons finely chopped fresh
coriander**

⅔ cup fresh breadcrumbs

⅓ cup finely grated Fontina cheese

½ teaspoon salt

**3 ounces cooked spinach, squeezed
and finely chopped**

1 pound ricotta

1 beaten egg

SAUCE

6 tablespoons butter

1 small zucchini, grated

salt and nutmeg

**fresh coriander leaves, cut into thin
strips, to garnish**

1 TO PREPARE PASTA: Pile flour on a work
surface, make a well in the center and add
salt and eggs. Using a fork, break up eggs
and begin to incorporate flour. Continue
blending flour until you have a loosely
formed mass of dough. Begin kneading with
your hands, adding more flour or a little
water if needed. Knead until you have a
smooth, elastic ball. Cover with a damp cloth
or plastic wrap and let rest for 30 minutes.

2 Divide the ball into four, then using a
rolling pin or pasta machine, roll each into a
very thin, even sheet. Rest, covered, for
12 to 15 minutes.

3 TO PREPARE FILLING: Combine all
ingredients except beaten egg, in a bowl and
mix well.

4 Using a 2 inch round cutter, cut circles from the sheets of pasta. Keep pasta covered when not being used to prevent drying. Working a few at a time, paint the rim of each circle with beaten egg, place a little filling in the center and fold over to form a half-moon shape. Press the sides together, seal with a fluted pastry wheel or the tines of a fork. As the agnolotti are completed, place them in a single layer and dust very lightly with flour. Simmer the agnolotti in boiling salted water for 3 to 4 minutes.

5 TO PREPARE SAUCE: Melt butter in a saucepan until golden, and then add zucchini. Stir over a very low heat until tender, season with salt and a pinch of nutmeg, and keep warm.

6 Drain agnolotti, transfer to a warm serving dish and top with zucchini. Sprinkle with sliced coriander and toss lightly before serving.

SERVES 4

TOMATO FETTUCCINE WITH CALAMARI (SQUID) AND SNOW PEAS

½ pound young calamari (squid), cleaned and cut into rings

milk

¾ pound fresh tomato fettuccine or ½ pound dried

3 tablespoons unsalted butter

dash cognac or brandy

10 small snow peas, trimmed and halved

salt and white pepper

1 to 2 pinches saffron

¾ cup heavy cream

1 Cover calamari rings with milk and soak for 45 minutes.

2 Cook fettuccine in boiling salted water.

3 Drain calamari, reserving milk, and sauté quickly in melted butter until tender, 1 to 2 minutes. Add cognac and cook, stirring, until evaporated. Add 4 tablespoons of the soaking milk and reduce slightly before adding the snow peas. Season with salt and pepper and add saffron, then cook briefly before adding cream. Heat until slightly thickened.

4 When fettuccine is *al dente*, drain, then transfer to warm plates. Spoon sauce over pasta and serve.

SERVES 4 AS AN APPETIZER OR LUNCHEON ENTRÉE

Tomato Fettuccine with Calamari (Squid) and Snow Peas (above) and Seafood Agnolotti with Coriander and Zucchini (below)

AFRICAN HERITAGE GIFT SHOP AND GALLERY

Saffron-flavored pasta is perfect to serve with seafood. A subtle cream-based sauce is a good complement and the caviar contributes little beads of saltiness as they're eaten. Use more or less caviar, depending on its quality.

SAFFRON PASTA WITH SCALLOPS AND BLACK CAVIAR

PASTA

good pinch of saffron

2 teaspoons warm water

3 cups sifted flour or 1½ cups sifted flour and ¾ cup semolina

large pinch salt

3 eggs

SAUCE

¾ pound fresh scallops, soaked in milk to cover for 30 minutes

2 tablespoons butter

salt and white pepper

1 to 2 teaspoons Pernod or Ricard

1¼ cups cream

1 tablespoon black caviar or lump fish roe

1 TO PREPARE PASTA: Mix saffron in water and set aside for 10 minutes. Combine flours and pile on a work surface, make a well in the center and add salt and eggs. Using a fork, break up eggs and begin to incorporate flour. Continue blending flour until you have a loosely formed mass of dough. Begin kneading with your hands, adding more flour or a little water if needed. Knead until you have a smooth, elastic ball. If preferred, the dough can be mixed in a food processor. Cover with a damp cloth or plastic wrap and let rest for 30 minutes.

2 Divide the ball into four, then using a rolling pin or pasta machine, roll each into long sheets of a thickness for tagliatelle. Rest, covered, for 12 to 15 minutes, then cut into strips about ¼ inch thick.

3 TO PREPARE SAUCE: Remove scallops from milk with a slotted spoon, reserving liquid. Melt butter in a frying pan and sauté scallops until just opaque. Season lightly, and add Pernod. Turn up the heat and cook, stirring, until most of the liquid has evaporated. Remove scallops and set aside.

Add cream to the pan and boil until thickened. Taste for seasoning, then stir in scallops, and set aside briefly in a warm place.

4 Meanwhile cook tagliarini in boiling salted water until *al dente*, about 1½ to 2 minutes. Drain, and quickly stir through a little vegetable oil before transferring to warmed plates. Spoon the sauce on top and sprinkle with caviar.

SERVES 4 AS AN APPETIZER OR LUNCHEON ENTRÉE

FRESH HERB FETTUCCINE WITH SMOKED SALMON AND ASPARAGUS

PASTA

2 cups sifted flour or 1½ cups flour and ¾ cup semolina

pinch salt

1 tablespoon finely chopped fresh parsley

1 tablespoon finely chopped fresh basil

2 eggs

SAUCE

¾ pound fresh asparagus spears, trimmed, peeled and halved

3 tablespoons butter

⅓ pound sliced smoked salmon, cut into strips

1 cup heavy cream

freshly ground black pepper

1 TO PREPARE PASTA: Pile flour and salt on a work surface and make a well in the middle. Using a fork, break up eggs and begin to incorporate eggs and herbs into the flour. Continue blending until you have a loosely formed mass of dough, then use your hands and knead it, adding a little flour or water if necessary for it to become smooth and elastic. Knead for at least 6 minutes and then rest, covered with plastic wrap or a damp cloth, for 30 minutes.

2 Divide the dough into two and roll each half into a thin, even sheet using a rolling pin or pasta machine. Rest again, covered, for 10 minutes before cutting the sheets into fettuccine. There is no need to cover again unless the pasta could dry out before cooking.

3 TO PREPARE SAUCE: Put the bottom halves of the asparagus in boiling water for a minute or so before adding tops, and cook until tender. Remove spears, but reserve water for cooking fettuccine. Rinse in cold water, drain again, and cut pieces into halves. Bring pot back to the boil, add more water if necessary, and begin cooking the fettuccine.

4 In a large pan melt butter and add smoked salmon. Sauté gently for 30 seconds before adding cream. Increase the heat slightly and when cream is thickened add a few grindings of black pepper and the asparagus.

5 When pasta is *al dente*, drain, transfer to a hot serving dish and top with the sauce. Toss gently, and serve with freshly grated Parmesan and more ground pepper.

SERVES 4 AS AN APPETIZER OR LUNCHEON ENTRÉE

≈ **FRESH HERB PASTA**

Pasta flavored with fresh herbs makes a wonderful base for light, fresh sauces. Herbs and vegetables which are in season at the same time, like the basil and asparagus in this recipe, often make perfect partners and require little else to flavor the dish. Along with the taste, the attractive appearance of green herbs through the pasta is reason enough to serve it with just melted butter and grated cheese. Try basil pasta with a cold sauce made from fresh ripe tomatoes, or fettuccine flavored with fresh sage coated with a creamy Gorgonzola sauce.

SWORDFISH WITH ZUCCHINI AND SAFFRON

3 zucchini, julienned

3 tablespoons unsalted butter

1 pound fresh swordfish or tuna fillets, cut into 1 to 2 inch slices

2 small onions, thinly sliced

1 clove garlic, crushed

pinch of saffron

½ teaspoon salt

½ teaspoon freshly ground black pepper

½ cup chicken stock

½ cup heavy cream

1¼ pounds fresh fettuccine or 1 pound dried

¼ teaspoon nutmeg

¼ teaspoon curry powder

1 Sprinkle zucchini with a little salt and let drain in a colander for 30 minutes.

2 Melt half the butter in a large pan and cook swordfish until just done. Remove from pan and set aside.

3 Add remaining butter to pan and sauté onions and garlic until soft, then stir in saffron and seasonings. Add stock and cream and reduce over a medium heat.

4 Begin cooking the fettuccine in boiling salted water.

5 When the sauce is smooth and thick, add drained zucchini and simmer for 1 minute. Add swordfish and heat through.

6 Drain pasta when it is *al dente*, transfer to a warm serving dish and pour over the sauce just before serving.

SERVES 4 AS AN APPETIZER OR LUNCHEON ENTRÉE

≈ **SAFFRON**

Saffron comes from the autumn crocus flower. It is usually sold by the gram in vials or packets. The strands should be steeped in a little water to draw out their flavor and color or can be lightly toasted to intensify the color.

≈ **RIGATE**

This term is used to describe pasta which is ridged or grooved. It helps the sauce cling to the pasta.

SHELLS STUFFED WITH BACON, SPINACH AND RICOTTA

To serve shells as an hors d'oeuvre, bake them at 350°F until the cheese is golden; this tends to give a firmer textured pasta which is easier to pick up with the finger. Cook a few more shells than needed, in case they tear during cooking.

12 giant pasta shells

1 teaspoon olive oil

1 clove garlic, crushed

3 ounces pancetta or bacon, cut into ½ pieces

4 canned Italian tomatoes, drained and pulped

1 tablespoon fresh breadcrumbs

¼ cup heavy cream

3½ cups ricotta cheese

½ pound finely chopped, well-drained, cooked spinach

1 teaspoon chopped fresh basil or ½ teaspoon dried

3 tablespoons grated Parmesan cheese

good pinch nutmeg

salt and freshly ground black pepper

extra grated Parmesan cheese

1 Cook pasta shells, stirring once or twice, until tender but firm. Drain, rinse under cold water and drain again. Set aside.

2 Heat oil in a frying pan and sauté garlic and bacon until slightly crisp.

3 Add tomato pulp, stir in breadcrumbs and cook briefly, then add cream. Cook 1 to 2 minutes more, stirring, until the mixture is quite dry.

4 Mix ricotta in a bowl with the bacon mixture, spinach, basil, Parmesan and nutmeg; blend well. Season with salt and pepper and a bit more nutmeg if desired.

5 Stuff each pasta shell with some of the filling and place them close together in a shallow heat-proof dish.

Shells Stuffed with Bacon, Spinach and Ricotta (above) and Pasta with Roasted Red Peppers

6 Sprinkle remaining filling and extra Parmesan over the top and place under a hot broiler until the cheese is melted and golden.

SERVES 4 AS AN APPETIZER OR LUNCHEON ENTRÉE

PASTA WITH ROASTED RED PEPPERS

5 large deep red peppers

¾ pound ridged pasta such as penne rigate, rotelli or conchiglie

3 tablespoons extra virgin olive oil

3 tablespoons olive oil

3 tablespoons finely chopped fresh basil or 3 tablespoons fresh parsley

3 anchovy fillets, drained and finely minced

2 cloves garlic, crushed

salt and freshly ground black pepper

1 Place peppers under a hot broiler and roast, turning occasionally, until the skins are charred and blistered. Remove and place in a large plastic bag, tied off, to sweat 30 minutes, when the charred pepper skins can be removed easily. Remove seeds and slice peppers into 2 inch lengths. Sprinkle with some extra virgin olive oil and set aside.

2 Heat olive oil in a frying pan and sauté basil, anchovies and garlic over low heat for 1 minute. Stir in peppers and season with salt and pepper. Add extra virgin olive oil and cook over a low heat to develop the flavor.

3 Cook pasta in boiling salted water. When *al dente*, drain and transfer to a serving bowl. Pour over peppers and toss thoroughly with a couple of chopped basil or parsley leaves.

SERVES 4

SALMON WITH LEMON CANNELLONI

TOMATO PASTA

3 cups sifted flour

pinch salt

2 eggs

2 tablespoons tomato paste

FILLING

2½ cups ricotta cheese

Two 14-ounce cans pink salmon, drained (reserve liquid)

juice 1 lemon

1 large egg, lightly beaten

3 tablespoons finely chopped onion

½ teaspoon salt

SAUCE

¼ pound butter

⅔ cup sifted flour

½ teaspoon salt

¼ teaspoon each white pepper and nutmeg

2¾ cups warmed milk

reserved liquid from salmon

grated rind 1 lemon

GARNISH

1 tablespoon chopped fresh dill

1 TO PREPARE PASTA: Sift flour and salt onto a work surface and make a well in the center. Lightly beat eggs with tomato paste and pour into flour well. Gradually work flour using a fork until a roughly combined dough is formed. Then begin kneading to obtain a smooth dough adding a little flour or water if necessary for it to become smooth and elastic. Shape into a ball, cover with plastic wrap or an upturned bowl, and rest for 30 minutes.

2 Divide dough into two and roll each half out into a thin, even sheet using a rolling pin or pasta machine. Trim into rectangles about 4 x 5 inches.

3 TO PREPARE FILLING: Place all ingredients in a bowl and combine well.

4 TO PREPARE SAUCE: Melt butter in a saucepan and stir in flour. Cook gently over low heat until roux is slightly colored. Stir in salt, pepper and nutmeg. Gradually pour in milk, stirring constantly, and cook until smooth and thick. Add reserved salmon liquid and lemon rind and set aside to cool.

5 Preheat oven to 350°F.

6 TO ASSEMBLE CANNELLONI: Cook the pasta sheets, a couple at a time, in boiling salted water until *al dente*. Remove with a large slotted spoon and layer on dry dish towels to drain. Trim edges to desired size. Put a thick line of filling along the length of each sheet and roll into tubes. Spread one-third of the sauce over the bottom of a shallow baking dish, and arrange cannelloni tubes side by side. Pour remaining sauce over the top, covering all exposed pasta. Sprinkle with chopped dill and bake until bubbly, about 30 minutes.

SERVES 4 AS AN APPETIZER OR LUNCHEON ENTRÉE

GORGONZOLA AND WALNUT RAVIOLI

PASTA

4¼ cups sifted flour

large pinch salt

4 eggs, beaten lightly

FILLING

2½ cups ricotta cheese

3 ounces Gorgonzola cheese

½ cup walnuts, chopped

½ cup grated Parmesan cheese

3 tablespoons toasted fresh breadcrumbs

1 beaten egg

SAUCE

3 tablespoons butter

½ cup heavy cream

grated Parmesan cheese

1 TO PREPARE PASTA: Sift flour and salt into a pile on a work surface, making a well in the middle. Add eggs and begin to incorporate the flour, using a fork. Continue until you have a loosely blended dough. Using your hands, knead the dough until smooth and elastic, about 6 minutes. Cover with plastic wrap or a damp cloth and let rest for 30 minutes.

2 Divide dough into four and, working one-quarter at a time, roll each into a very thin, even sheet, using a rolling pin or pasta machine. Rest the sheets of pasta, covered, while you make the filling.

3 TO PREPARE FILLING: Combine all ingredients except egg in a food processor or blender and mix until a coarse paste is obtained.

4 Working 1 sheet of pasta at a time, cut out 2 inch squares and put a little filling in the center of each. Paint round the rims with beaten egg, then fold over diagonally to form triangles and press the cut edges together. Trim the cut edge with a fluted pastry wheel or tines of a fork, then put aside in a single layer until the rest are completed.

5 In a large pot of boiling, salted and oiled water poach the ravioli, a few at a time, until done, about 4 minutes. Drain and transfer to a warm serving dish.

6 TO PREPARE SAUCE: Melt butter, add cream and simmer until slightly thickened. Pour over ravioli, add 1 or 2 tablespoons of Parmesan, and toss lightly before serving. Serve with extra Parmesan and freshly ground black pepper.

SERVES 4

PORK AND VEAL TERRINE

1 cup ditalini or other very small pasta

1 small green pepper, seeded and roughly chopped

⅔ cup carrots, peeled and sliced

4 cloves garlic

2 onions, roughly chopped

2 tablespoons chopped fresh parsley

8 slices bacon

1 heaped teaspoon dried thyme

1½ pounds each ground pork and veal

¾ cup fresh breadcrumbs

2 eggs, lightly beaten

1 teaspoon nutmeg

salt and freshly ground black pepper

1 Cook pasta in boiling salted water until *al dente*. Drain, rinse under cold water, then drain again.

2 Preheat oven to 350°F.

3 Put pepper, carrots, garlic, onion and parsley into a food processor or blender and process until they are chopped finely, almost a purée. Transfer mixture into a large bowl.

4 Finely chop 2 bacon slices by hand, and add them to the bowl with thyme, the ground meat, breadcrumbs and eggs. Combine lightly, then add nutmeg, generous shakings of salt and pepper, and lastly the pasta. Mix thoroughly.

5 Shape into a fat log and wrap loosely but evenly with remaining bacon. Place in a shallow baking dish and bake for 1½ hours.

SERVES 6 TO 8

≈ **PORK AND VEAL TERRINE**
This loaf is as good cold as hot so it's an ideal choice for a picnic. It keeps well and slices beautifully as a tasty crust forms during baking.

≈ **CHICKEN ROLLS WITH PAGLIA E FIENO**

This dish looks splendid and is a great hit when served for a supper; the chicken rolls can be prepared earlier in the day to leave only the pasta for last-minute cooking.

Chicken Rolls with Paglia e Fieno

CHICKEN ROLLS WITH PAGLIA E FIENO

4 chicken fillets

3 ounces minced prosciutto or raw smoked ham

3½ tablespoons softened butter

6 canned artichoke hearts, drained and quartered

salt and freshly ground black pepper

sifted flour

3 tablespoons olive oil

1 small onion, finely chopped

½ cup dry white wine

⅔ cup chicken stock

½ pound each fresh fettuccine and spinach fettuccine or ¾ pound dried mixed

2 to 3 sprigs fresh bay or lemon leaves

freshly grated Parmesan cheese

1 Flatten each chicken fillet with a mallet, being careful not to tear the flesh. Mix prosciutto with half the butter and spread this mixture over the chicken slices. Top each with sections of artichoke heart, season, roll up around the stuffing, and skewer or tie tightly.

2 Heat olive oil and remaining butter in a flame-proof casserole dish and gently sauté onion for 5 minutes. Add chicken rolls and brown on all sides. Add wine, and cook briefly to evaporate a little. Season to taste, lower heat and cook, covered, for about 30 minutes or until meat is tender. Moisten occasionally with stock to make a sauce. Adjust seasoning if necessary.

3 Cook fettuccine in boiling salted water until *al dente*, drain and stir through a little olive oil. Transfer to a warm serving dish,

VILLA ITALIANA

and toss with sauce from the chicken.

4 Remove skewers or string from the chicken rolls, arrange them with the pasta and decorate the dish with bay or lemon leaves. Serve immediately with freshly grated Parmesan.

SERVES 4

SPANISH STYLE FRESH TUNA AND LASAGNETTE

1½ tablespoons olive oil

1½ pounds fresh tuna, or swordfish

2 ounces prosciutto or unsmoked bacon, chopped

½ cup white wine

3 medium-sized onions, cut in quarters

2 cloves garlic, cut in half

¾ pound lasagnette, broken in half

1 tablespoon grated baking chocolate

1 tablespoon dried breadcrumbs

1 cup veal stock

celery leaves, to garnish

1 Put olive oil in the bottom of a heavy pot, add tuna and top with prosciutto or bacon, wine, onions and garlic. Cook over medium heat 5 minutes, turn and cook for another 5 minutes. Lower heat and cook, covered, for 1½ to 2 hours.

2 Cook lasagnette in boiling salted water 20 minutes before serving.

3 Remove fish from the pot and keep warm. Stir stock, chocolate, and breadcrumbs with the remaining ingredients in the pot, and bring to the boil. Simmer 4 to 5 minutes, and strain through a fine sieve. If a thicker sauce is desired, transfer to a small saucepan and reduce quickly.

4 When pasta is *al dente*, drain and transfer to a warm serving dish. Top with pieces of fish, pour over sauce and serve with celery leaves scattered on top.

SERVES 4

TAGLIATELLE WITH ASPARAGUS, HAM AND CREAM

1 pound fresh asparagus

salt

1 pound fresh tagliatelle or ¾ pound dried

3½ tablespoons butter

½ pound prosciutto or unsmoked ham, cut into 1 inch strips

1 cup heavy cream

freshly ground black pepper

3 tablespoons freshly grated Parmesan cheese

1 Put a large pan of water on to boil.

2 Peel asparagus, and break off tough bottoms. Cut off tips at about 2 inches, but keep stalks in one piece.

3 Salt boiling water, add asparagus stalks, thickest ones first, and boil until half done. Add tips and continue boiling until tender but still crisp, stiff and bright green. Test as you go along. Remove and cool slightly.

4 Cook the pasta in the asparagus water. Melt butter in a frying pan and sauté prosciutto until the butter begins to brown, but don't crisp the prosciutto. Add cream and bring back to the boil, scraping the prosciutto bits off the bottom. Grind in some fresh pepper.

5 Slice asparagus stalks into 2 inch lengths. Add to the sauce with the tops and stir to coat; the cream should have reduced and thickened.

6 Drain pasta when it is *al dente* and turn into a warm serving bowl. Mix in the sauce and the Parmesan, toss gently, and taste for salt and pepper before serving.

SERVES 4

≈ **CHOCOLATE**

In some parts of Spain, chocolate is often used to flavor fish dishes. Only a little is used, but the resulting sauce has a smooth mellow taste. There is a theory that this practice originated when Spanish sailors first brought chocolate to Europe.

≈ **TAGLIATELLE WITH ASPARAGUS, HAM AND CREAM**

Asparagus, Parmesan, butter and black pepper: there's no better combination of flavors and I can't think of any way to improve this dish, unless it were to beat an egg with the Parmesan and stir this through at the last minute.

≈ **ITALIAN TOMATOES**

Italian peeled tomatoes are recommended because they are deep red and ripe, sweet and full of flavor, and they are canned in thick natural purée which can be used elsewhere. However, it's a matter of shopping around and finding the brand you like.

BAKED TORTELLINI WITH EGGPLANT AND POTATO

1 small eggplant, cut into ¾ inch dice

½ pound beef or cheese tortellini

½ pound potatoes, peeled and cut into ¾ inch thick slices

½ cup olive oil

1 onion, thinly sliced

One 14-ounce can Italian peeled tomatoes

½ teaspoon chopped fresh oregano or ¼ teaspoon dried

pinch cayenne pepper

salt and freshly ground black pepper

¾ cup Fontina cheese, shredded

3 tablespoons extra chopped fresh oregano or parsley

1 Preheat oven to 375°F.

2 Sprinkle eggplant with salt and drain in a colander or strainer.

3 Cook tortellini, drain and place in a shallow ovenproof dish.

4 Boil potatoes until just cooked. Drain. Sauté potatoes in some of the oil until brown, then add to the tortellini.

5 With a little more oil, sauté onion gently for 5 minutes, then add drained eggplant. Continue cooking (adding more oil if necessary), until eggplant is tender and golden.

6 Lightly drain tomatoes and add to the pan, breaking them up with a wooden spoon. Add oregano, cayenne, salt and pepper. Cook until the tomatoes have reduced and there is little liquid left.

7 Add to the dish with the tortellini and toss through with one-third of the Fontina. Season again with a few grinds of black pepper and salt. Distribute the remaining Fontina over the top and sprinkle with the extra oregano or parsley.

8 Bake 10 minutes until hot and bubbly.

SERVES 4

BUCATINI WITH TOMATOES AND SEAFOOD

1½ tablespoons butter

2 tablespoons olive oil

1 onion, finely chopped

3 cloves garlic, crushed

1 teaspoon finely chopped fresh parsley

good pinch thyme

One 35-ounce can chopped or puréed Italian tomatoes

salt and freshly ground black pepper

¾ cup fish stock or water

12 fresh or canned baby clams, cleaned

⅓ pound cleaned calamari (squid), sliced into rings

⅓ pound shrimp, cut into pieces

⅓ pound white fish fillets, cut into pieces

½ to 2 teaspoons turmeric, to taste

pinch of saffron (optional)

dash Pernod or Ricard (optional)

1 pound bucatini

1 Melt butter and oil in a large pot and sauté onion and garlic over a low heat for 5 minutes. Add parsley and thyme, and stir in tomatoes. Season with salt and pepper, raise heat slightly and cook, covered, for 15 minutes.

2 Remove lid and cook another 5 to 10 minutes, or until the sauce thickens. Add stock and bring to the boil. Add remaining ingredients and simmer until clams open and the seafood is cooked. Adjust seasoning. Discard any clams which have not opened.

3 Cook bucatini in boiling salted water. When *al dente*, drain and transfer to a heated serving dish, and top with the sauce. (As a rule, cheese is not served with seafood sauces.)

SERVES 4

Baked Tortellini with Eggplant and Potato

≈ OLIVE OIL

Pure olive oil is chemically treated and blended, but only with other olive oils. It contains no cholesterol. Extra virgin olive oil is generally made from the first pressing of slightly underripe olives, and sometimes produced without chemical means.

BAKED EGGPLANT AND WHOLE WHEAT FETTUCCINE

1 pound fresh whole wheat fettuccine or ⅔ pound dried

2 eggplants cut into ½ inch slices

salt and freshly ground black pepper

⅓ cup olive oil

1 onion, chopped

1 clove garlic, crushed

1 pound fresh tomatoes, peeled, seeded and chopped

1 tablespoon chopped fresh basil or 1 teaspoon dried

4 zucchini, sliced

½ pound mushrooms, sliced

3 tablespoons wheatgerm

3 tablespoons chopped fresh parsley

½ pound mozzarella cheese, sliced

½ cup heavy cream

1 Break fettuccine into thirds and cook in boiling salted water until *al dente*. Drain and stir with a little olive oil to prevent sticking. Set aside.

2 Lightly sprinkle eggplant slices with salt and drain for 30 minutes.

3 Heat half the oil in a saucepan and gently sauté onion and garlic for 5 minutes. Add tomatoes, basil, salt and pepper and simmer, uncovered, until the sauce has thickened; about 12 minutes.

4 Preheat oven to 350°F.

5 Drain and dry eggplant. Heat remaining oil in a frying pan and sauté eggplant slices until golden, then remove. Cook zucchini, mushrooms and wheatgerm until tender, and then combine with the eggplant.

6 Arrange half the fettuccine in the bottom of a greased deep baking dish. Sprinkle with half the parsley, then arrange half the eggplant mixture on this, and pour over half the tomato sauce. Repeat layering, and cover the last level of tomatoes with the mozzarella slices. Pour cream on the top and bake, uncovered, for 30 minutes.

SERVES 4 TO 6

TAGLIERINI WITH SARDINES

1 small whole fennel

12 fresh sardines, about 5 inches long, cleaned and split open

½ cup sifted flour, seasoned with salt and pepper

½ cup olive oil

1 small onion, finely chopped

1 anchovy fillet, chopped

3 tablespoons toasted pine nuts

1 tablespoon golden raisins

pinch saffron

freshly ground black pepper

1 pound mixed fresh spinach and plain taglierini or ¾ pound dried

1 Cut fennel top, chop greens and reserve. Trim the bulb, discarding any tough outer stalks, and finely slice enough to fill one-third of a cup. Save the rest for another use.

2 Toss sardines in seasoned flour and fry them very gently in half the olive oil, a few at a time. Be careful not to break them when turning, remove and keep warm.

3 Heat remaining oil and sauté onion and fennel until soft. Mash in anchovy and cook another 30 seconds. Add pine nuts, sultanas, saffron and a little black pepper. Stir and keep warm.

4 Cook taglierini in boiling salted water until *al dente*. Drain and put in a warm serving dish. Add the fennel sauce, toss through, and place sardines on top. Sprinkle with fennel greens and serve immediately.

SERVES 4

SPAGHETTI WITH CALAMARI

1¾ pounds fresh baby calamari (squid)

⅓ cup olive oil

1 large onion, finely chopped

3 cloves garlic, crushed

pinch red pepper flakes

One 28-ounce can Italian peeled tomatoes, drained and chopped

salt and freshly ground black pepper

1½ pounds fresh spaghetti or 1 pound dried

3 tablespoons chopped fresh coriander

1 Remove head from squid and cut the tentacles straight across above the eyes. Discard head, keep tentacles and body, squeezing out the bony beak. If tentacles are too large, cut in two. Remove the thin bone, rinse sacs under cold water, and peel off the outer thin skin of each sac at the same time. If sacs seem too large, cut them into sections.

2 Heat oil and gently sauté onion, garlic and red pepper flakes, until onion is soft and golden.

3 Add squid and cook until they turn opaque. Add tomatoes and season with salt and pepper. Stir well, then lower heat and cook, covered, for 30 minutes.

4 Cook spaghetti in boiling salted water until *al dente*. Drain and transfer to a warm serving bowl. Pour over sauce and toss through coriander just before serving.

SERVES 4

SPAGHETTI WITH CLAMS

2 pounds small clams, washed and scrubbed

1 cup dry white wine

1 cup water

⅓ cup olive oil

2 cloves garlic, crushed

1 onion, finely chopped

One 28-ounce can Italian peeled tomatoes, drained and chopped

3 tablespoons finely chopped fresh parsley

pinch red pepper flakes

3½ tablespoons butter

salt and freshly ground black pepper

1½ pounds fresh spaghetti or 1 pound dried

1 Place clams in a large pan with wine, water and 1 tablespoon oil. Cover and cook over a high heat. As the clams open remove them with a slotted spoon; discard those which don't open. Continue boiling liquid until roughly 1 cup remains; strain through cheesecloth and set aside.

2 In a large pan heat remaining oil and sauté garlic and onion until golden. Add clam liquid and let it evaporate a little before adding tomatoes, parsley, red pepper flakes and butter. Cook, uncovered, for 10 minutes over a medium heat. Season sauce and add a little more wine if it becomes too thick. Add clams and stir to heat.

3 Cook spaghetti in boiling salted water. When it is *al dente*, drain, and stir in a little olive oil to prevent sticking.

4 Transfer to warm bowls, top with sauce and serve with a small slice of butter on top of each dish, but no cheese.

SERVES 4

VILLA ITALIANA

Spaghetti with Clams

≈ SPAGHETTI WITH CLAMS

Other shellfish can be included in the sauce, and the red pepper flakes can be left out if a less spicy dish is preferred. If only large clams are available, prepare them as indicated, but remove the meat and discard most of the shells, saving just a few for decoration.

SHELLS AND SHELLFISH SALAD

1 pound medium-sized conchiglie

1⅓ cups mayonnaise, preferably homemade

**¼ cup chopped fresh tarragon or
2½ tablespoons dried**

2 tablespoons finely chopped fresh parsley

red pepper flakes

fresh lemon juice

**2 pounds cooked shellfish: shrimp, lobster,
crabmeat, or a combination,
cut into bite-sized pieces**

2 radishes, sliced

½ green pepper, julienned

salt and freshly ground black pepper

*Shells and Shellfish
Salad*

1 Cook pasta in boiling salted water until *al dente*. Drain, rinse under cold water and drain again. Place in a large bowl and stir through 1 to 2 tablespoons of mayonnaise. Cool to room temperature, stirring occasionally to prevent sticking.

2 If using dried tarragon, simmer in ¼ cup milk for 3 to 4 minutes; drain. Combine tarragon, parsley, red pepper flakes, lemon juice and remaining mayonnaise and mix well.

3 Add shellfish to pasta with most of the radishes and pepper, and salt and pepper. Mix through the tarragon mayonnaise and toss gently to coat. Cover, and chill before serving, adding more mayonnaise if the mixture is a little dry. Decorate with remaining radish and pepper slices.

**SERVES 8 AS A FIRST COURSE,
4 AS A MAIN MEAL**

≈ PARSLEY

The parsley with the best flavor and leaf is the flat-leafed Italian variety. Dried parsley is simply not a good alternative in any recipe requiring fresh parsley.

LASAGNE WITH SHRIMP AND ARTICHOKE HEARTS

One 28-ounce can Italian peeled tomatoes, drained and pulped

1 clove garlic, crushed

salt and freshly ground black pepper

pinch red pepper flakes

½ teaspoon finely chopped fresh basil or ¼ teaspoon dried

¼ cup olive oil

½ pound dried lasagne sheets or ¾ pound fresh

¾ pound shelled cooked shrimp, halved if large

6 canned artichoke hearts, each cut into 6 pieces

3 tablespoons chopped fresh parsley

¼ pound mozzarella cheese, sliced

8 to 10 anchovy fillets

1 Preheat oven to 400°F.

2 Put tomatoes, garlic, salt, pepper, red pepper flakes, basil and olive oil in a shallow ovenproof dish. Stir to combine and bake for 25 to 30 minutes.

3 While the tomato sauce is baking, cook lasagne sheets until *al dente*; and drain in one layer on dry dish towels.

4 TO ASSEMBLE LASAGNE: Grease a rectangular baking dish or lasagne pan. Put a thin layer of tomato sauce on the bottom and cover with a single layer of pasta. Combine the rest of the tomato sauce with shrimp, artichoke hearts, parsley, salt and pepper. Now alternate layers of sauce and pasta, finishing with a layer of sauce. Cover this with slices of mozzarella and top with a lattice pattern of anchovies.

5 Lower heat to 350°F and bake for 40 minutes, or until golden on top.

SERVES 4

ROAST BEEF WITH ROTELLI

½ cup olive oil

3½ tablespoons butter

4½ pounds of onions, thinly sliced

2½ pounds beef chuck roast, bottom round or brisket

¼ pound diced pancetta or bacon

1 stalk celery, chopped

1 carrot, chopped

sprig fresh marjoram or ½ teaspoon dried

salt and freshly ground black pepper

1 cup dry white wine

3 tablespoons water, beef stock or cream

1¼ pounds fresh rotelli or ¾ pound dried

freshly grated Parmesan, to serve

1 Preheat oven to 300°F.

2 Melt butter and 3 tablespoons oil in a large Dutch oven. Add onions and sauté over a low heat until golden and tender, at least 15 minutes. Remove and set aside.

3 Heat remaining oil in the pot and brown the roast on all sides. Add pancetta or bacon and fry for a short time before adding celery and carrot, marjoram, salt and pepper. Cook for 1 to 2 minutes more, then return onions to the pot with half the wine. Stir well and cook for a minute until the raw wine aroma dissipates, then cover the pot and transfer to the oven.

4 Bake for 2 to 2½ hours or until the meat is tender. Add more wine as the juices reduce. A rich, dark gravy should surround the beef. Transfer the meat to a carving tray and keep warm.

5 Take 1¾ cups of the gravy and place in a blender or food processor with 3 tablespoons of water, beef stock or cream. Blend until sauce is smooth and thick. Transfer to a small saucepan to keep hot.

6 Cook pasta in boiling salted water. Drain and serve with the onion sauce and freshly grated Parmesan as the first course. Carve the beef and serve with its gravy for the entrée.

SERVES 5 TO 6

≈ ROAST BEEF WITH ROTELLI

The beef is also delicious served with a hot fresh tomato sauce instead of the gravy. Tiny yellow and green pattypan squash are an attractive vegetable to serve as an accompaniment; potatoes are not usually served with the main course.

*This chicken is excellent
served cold on a picnic.
The flesh remains moist
and succulent and the
stuffing becomes a side
salad. The bacon
which didn't burn
during the roasting can
be crumbled and used in
other dishes, e.g. tossed
through a green salad or
used as flavoring in a
pasta sauce.*

ROAST CHICKEN WITH PASTA STUFFING

1½ cups small shaped dried pasta (pennete or ditali)

12 scallions, white parts only, thinly sliced

12 pistachio nuts, shelled

3 tablespoons finely chopped mixed fresh herbs (parsley, basil, sage or oregano)

5 canned Italian peeled tomatoes, drained and pulped

1 thick slice of bacon, cut into small pieces

¼ teaspoon salt

½ teaspoon freshly ground black pepper

3½ tablespoons butter, softened

One 2½ to 3 pound fresh chicken, or two Cornish hens

1 slice bread

4 extra bacon slices

1 Cook pasta until three-quarters done then drain.

2 Preheat oven to 425°F.

3 In a large bowl combine scallions, pistachio nuts, herbs, tomatoes, diced bacon, salt and pepper with the pasta.

4 Using half the butter, grease the inside of the chicken, and fill it with the pasta stuffing. Place a slice of bread inside the opening to keep the stuffing in, and truss the bird. (If using Cornish hens, divide the ingredients between them.)

5 Rub the chicken over with the remaining butter and place it on its side on a rack in a baking dish. Sprinkle the body with a little ground black pepper and cover it with the extra bacon slices. Roast for 20 minutes.

6 Turn the bird over onto its other side, sprinkle over a little more ground black pepper, cover with the bacon and put back into the oven for a further 20 minutes.

7 Remove bacon, turn the bird onto its back and roast again, basting often with the juices in the dish. After 20 minutes test to see if the chicken is cooked. If a skewer pushed into the thick flesh of a thigh produces liquid with a red tinge, roast the bird another 5 minutes and test again. When the juices come clear the chicken is done. Rest it for a couple of minutes in a warm place before carving.

SERVES 2

FUSILLI AND SNAPPER BAKED IN FOIL

1 cup fusilli

6 tablespoons butter

1 clove garlic

1 red pepper, cut into strips

1½ pounds snapper fillets or other white fleshed fish, cut into bite-sized pieces

¼ pound mushrooms, sliced

1 tablespoon each chopped fresh parsley and fresh dill

salt and freshly ground black pepper

½ cup heavy cream

3 tablespoons dry white wine

1 Cook fusilli in boiling salted water until not quite *al dente*. Drain and stir through a little vegetable oil to prevent sticking.

2 Sauté garlic clove and pepper in butter for 2 minutes. Add snapper fillets and cook until just opaque. Add mushrooms, sauté briefly and then discard garlic. Stir in parsley and dill, season well and add cream. Cook until cream bubbles and then stir in the fusilli.

3 Preheat oven to 400°F.

4 Divide the mixture among four large sheets of greased aluminium foil or parchment paper. Season again, lightly sprinkle each with wine and fold up parcels, sealing well to prevent steam from escaping. Place in a large shallow baking dish and bake for 20 minutes. Open carefully to let the steam out and serve immediately.

SERVES 4

SPAGHETTI WITH LAMB AND RED PEPPER

3½ tablespoons butter

3 tablespoons olive oil

3 red peppers, cut into thin strips
1 to 2 inches long

1 onion, finely chopped

3 cloves garlic, crushed

1¼ pounds lamb, preferably from the leg,
cut into small dice

1 tablespoon vinegar

One 14-ounce can Italian peeled tomatoes,
drained and chopped

¼ teaspoon red pepper flakes

salt

dry white wine

1½ pounds fresh spaghetti or 1 pound dried

½ cup grated Pecorino cheese

1 to 2 tablespoons finely chopped
fresh parsley

1 In a heavy-based casserole heat half the butter and oil and gently sauté peppers for 5 minutes. Remove with a slotted spoon and set aside.

2 Add remaining butter and oil to the pot and sauté onion, garlic and lamb over a medium heat until the lamb is lightly browned. Stir in vinegar, cover and leave for 10 minutes before proceeding.

3 Add tomatoes, red pepper flakes and cooked pepper, season with salt and cook the sauce for 5 minutes. Lower the heat and cook, covered, for a further 30 minutes, stirring once or twice. Add a little wine from time to time if the sauce begins to dry. Adjust seasoning if necessary.

4 Cook spaghetti in boiling salted water until *al dente*. Drain, and transfer to a warm serving dish. Pour over sauce and add grated Pecorino and parsley. Toss together lightly and serve with extra Pecorino.

SERVES 4 AS A MAIN COURSE

≈ **RED PEPPERS**

The darker the color, the sweeter and more concentrated the flavor, especially if broiled or roasted.

≈ **PECORINO CHEESE**

This was originally made from sheep's milk. It is sharper and more piquant than Parmesan.

RIGATONI WITH SAUSAGE AND FRESH MARJORAM

1½ tablespoons butter

2 tablespoons olive oil

1 onion, chopped

1 carrot, julienned

1 bay leaf

⅓ cup chopped bacon

½ pound spicy hard Italian sausage, skinned and sliced

One 14-ounce can Italian peeled tomatoes

salt and freshly ground black pepper

½ cup beef or chicken stock

1 pound rigatoni

1 heaping tablespoon chopped fresh marjoram or oregano

1 Cook onion, carrot and bay leaf in butter and oil until onion is transparent.

2 Add bacon and sausage and cook, stirring often, until brown.

3 Squeeze dry half the tomatoes, chop, and add to the pan. Add the rest whole and break up loosely with the spoon while stirring. Season well with salt and pepper and simmer for 30 minutes over a low heat, gradually adding stock as sauce dries.

4 Cook rigatoni in boiling salted water until *al dente*. Drain and transfer to a warm serving dish. Add marjoram and sauce, and toss together lightly before serving.

SERVES 4

ININI OF NEUTRAL BAY

Rigatoni with Sausage and Fresh Marjoram

≈ RIGATONI WITH SAUSAGE AND FRESH MARJORAM

The success of this sauce depends upon the quality of the sausages, and on fresh marjoram being used. The flavor is rich and spicy, and the appearance should be fresh and bright.

BAKED SNAPPER AND PENNE WITH LEMON, LIME OR ORANGE SAUCE

½ pound penne

½ cup vegetable oil

4 small to medium snapper steaks or other white-fleshed fish, trimmed

2 to 3 cloves garlic, crushed

1½ tablespoons chopped fresh coriander, plus some sprigs for decoration

⅔ cup tomato purée or juice from canned Italian peeled tomatoes

3 tablespoons fresh: lime, lemon, or orange juice, or a combination

red pepper flakes

1 Cook penne in boiling salted water until barely *al dente*. Drain and stir through a little vegetable oil to prevent sticking. Transfer to an ovenproof dish.

2 In a pan heat some of the oil and brown snapper on both sides. Transfer to the dish and lay side by side on top of the penne, covering it completely.

3 Preheat oven to 425°F.

4 Add remaining oil to the pan and gently sauté garlic. Stir in chopped coriander, tomato purée and citrus juice. Cook, stirring, until the sauce boils and gives off a citrus aroma.

5 Sprinkle in red pepper flakes to taste, and spoon sauce over snapper. Pour in a little water, about 3 tablespoons, to make sure all the pasta is moistened. Cover loosely with foil and bake for 25 to 30 minutes, or until snapper is tender. Decorate with coriander sprigs and serve from the dish.

SERVES 4

MEAT ROLL STUFFED WITH SPINACH AND HAM

MEAT MIXTURE

2 pounds lean ground beef

2 eggs, beaten

1 teaspoon thyme

½ teaspoon each salt, black pepper and crushed garlic

1 onion, finely chopped

3 tablespoons finely chopped fresh parsley

½ cup dried breadcrumbs

½ cup Marsala

1 teaspoon tomato paste

SPINACH MIXTURE

1 cup well-drained, cooked spinach, finely chopped

1 cup cooked stellini or other tiny interestingly shaped pasta

½ cup grated Cheddar cheese

2 tablespoons grated Parmesan cheese

¼ teaspoon each salt, pepper and nutmeg

3 ounces minced ham

TOPPING

¼ cup fresh breadcrumbs mixed with ¼ cup grated Parmesan

1 TO PREPARE MEAT MIXTURE: Thoroughly combine ingredients in a bowl.

2 TO PREPARE SPINACH MIXTURE: Combine ingredients well in another bowl.

3 Preheat oven to 350°F.

4 To assemble the roll, on a large sheet of foil flatten meat mixture into a rectangle approximately ½ inch thick, 15 inches long and 8 inches wide. Spread spinach mixture evenly over the top. Roll up, starting at one of the shorter sides and using the foil to lift and roll.

5 Sprinkle topping over loaf and wrap tightly in foil. Place in a small deep-sided baking dish and bake for 1½ hours. Rest for 5 minutes, still in the foil, before serving.

SERVES 6 TO 8

≈ **MEAT ROLL STUFFED WITH SPINACH AND HAM**

When served hot this loaf hardly requires a sauce as it is moist and succulent. Cold, it slices well for picnics and makes delicious sandwiches.

ZUCCHINI AND SAUSAGE LASAGNE

½ cup olive oil

2 small carrots, finely chopped

1 onion, finely chopped

2 stalks celery, finely chopped

½ pound hot Italian sausages

⅔ cup dry white wine

One 28-ounce can Italian peeled tomatoes, drained and chopped

salt and freshly ground black pepper

8 small zucchini sliced

½ teaspoon chopped fresh oregano or ¼ teaspoon dried

1 pound lasagne sheets

½ pound shredded Fontina cheese

¾ cup grated Parmesan cheese

1 Gently sauté carrots, onion and celery in half the oil until soft.

2 Remove casings from sausages and discard. Add meat to the pan and break up with a wooden spoon when stirring. Cook until brown, then pour in wine. Increase heat and cook until juices have reduced by half.

3 Add tomatoes, lower heat and simmer for 40 minutes, stirring from time to time. Season to taste.

4 In a separate pan, heat the remaining oil and sauté zucchini with a little salt and oregano until tender and golden.

5 Cook lasagne according to instructions and drain on dry dish towels.

6 Preheat oven to 375°F.

7 Place a layer of pasta in a greased lasagne pan, or other deep baking dish. Add a thin layer of sauce then some zucchini slices. Sprinkle with some Fontina and Parmesan cheese. Continue this layering until all ingredients are used up, finishing with Fontina and Parmesan. Bake for 30 minutes.

SERVES 6 TO 8 AS A MAIN MEAL

TAGLIATELLE WITH VEAL, WINE AND CREAM

Rich and filling, this dish makes an ideal meal served with a mixed salad. For a lighter sauce, the cream can be omitted and it's just as delicious.

1¼ pounds veal scallopine or escalopes, cut into strips

sifted flour seasoned with salt and pepper

3½ tablespoons butter

1 onion, sliced

½ cup dry white wine

4 to 5 tablespoons beef or chicken stock

⅔ cup heavy cream

salt and freshly ground black pepper

1½ pounds fresh tagliatelle or 1 pound dried

freshly grated Parmesan cheese

1 Coat pieces of veal with seasoned flour and sauté quickly in melted butter until browned. Remove with a slotted spoon and set aside.

2 Add onion to the pan and sauté gently until soft and golden, 8 to 10 minutes. Pour in wine and cook rapidly until the raw wine smell disappears, then add stock and cream and season with salt and pepper. Reduce again, and add veal towards the end.

3 Cook tagliatelle in boiling salted water until *al dente*. Drain and transfer to a warm serving dish.

4 Check the sauce for salt and pepper, stir in about 1 tablespoon Parmesan, pour over the pasta and toss through. Serve with extra grated Parmesan.

SERVES 4

Tagliatelle with Veal, Wine and Cream

ENDINGS

At the end of the day or the end of a meal, pasta works beautifully. With interesting textures and tastes of its own, it also provides the perfect foil for other flavors. In this section we have included recipes for luscious desserts, light suppers and delicious midnight snacks.

PASTA SOUFFLÉ

3 cups milk
grated rind ½ small lemon
2 teaspoons salt
½ pound spaghetti or tagliatelle
6 tablespoons softened butter
¾ cup sugar
3 large eggs, separated
**½ cup golden raisins, soaked
in ¼ cup brandy**
¾ cup chopped blanched almonds
pinch ground cinnamon

1 Preheat oven to 375°F.

2 Put milk, lemon rind and salt in a large saucepan and bring to the boil. Add pasta and gently cook, covered, until the pasta is tender, about 8 minutes. Remove the lid and set the pan in cold water to cool.

3 Cream butter and sugar together until smooth and light. Add egg yolks one at a time, beating well after each addition. Combine this mixture with milk and pasta, raisins and brandy, almonds, and cinnamon.

4 Beat egg whites until stiff and loosely fold into the pasta mixture. Turn into a large buttered soufflé dish and bake for 45 to 60 minutes. The top should be lightly browned and the center set or, if preferred, slightly custardy.

SERVES 4 TO 6

NEUTRAL COUNTRY

SWEET PASTA CAKE

⅔ pound fresh spaghetti or ½ pound dried

2 tablespoons butter

3 tablespoons sugar

⅓ cup mixed peel

⅓ cup golden raisins

¼ cup almonds

¼ cup dried figs or dates, chopped

3 tablespoons glacé cherries, chopped

3 tablespoons sifted flour

½ teaspoon cinnamon

2 eggs, beaten

1 Cook pasta in boiling salted water until *al dente*. Drain, rinse under cold water and drain again. Transfer to a bowl.

2 Preheat oven to 350°F.

3 Melt butter in a small saucepan. Add sugar and heat, stirring, until sugar dissolves. Leave to cool.

4 In a large bowl, thoroughly combine mixed peel, raisins, almonds, figs, glacé cherries, flour and cinnamon. Stir into cooked pasta, then add butter-sugar mixture and eggs. Blend well.

5 Transfer mixture to a greased 8-inch baking dish and smooth the top. Bake until set and golden, about 35 minutes. If the top browns, cover loosely with foil. When done, remove from oven and cool for 20 minutes before turning out.

SERVES 6 TO 8

CHESTNUT AGNOLOTTI

1½ pounds moist fresh pasta sheets, thinly rolled

FILLING

1 pound chestnut purée

3 tablespoons honey

3 tablespoons cocoa powder

3 tablespoons ground almonds

1 teaspoon cinnamon

1 teaspoon vanilla

3 teaspoons rum

¼ cup mixed peel, finely chopped

¾ cup fresh breadcrumbs

1½ tablespoons sugar

TO ASSEMBLE

beaten egg for sealing

vegetable oil for frying

melted honey and confectioner's sugar

1 TO PREPARE FILLING: In a bowl blend all ingredients to form a smooth paste.

2 Working one sheet of pasta at a time and using a cookie cutter, cut out circles about 2½ inches in diameter. Paint rims with beaten egg, then place some filling to one side of center. Fold the pasta over to form a half-moon shape, and press the edges together. Seal with a fluted pastry wheel or tines of a fork, and set aside in single layers.

3 When all are made, heat some oil about ½-inch deep in a shallow frying pan until a slight haze is visible. Fry agnolotti, a few at a time, until golden on both sides. Remove with a slotted spoon and drain on absorbent paper. Serve warm with honey drizzled over the top and sprinkle with confectioner's sugar.

SERVES 4

SWEET RICOTTA AND FUSILLI

½ pound fusilli

¾ cup ricotta cheese

pinch salt

1 tablespoon sugar

¼ teaspoon vanilla

¼ teaspoon grated lemon rind

¼ teaspoon cinnamon

heated milk

julienned lemon rind for decoration

1 Cook fusilli until *al dente*.

2 In a bowl, blend ricotta, pinch salt, sugar, vanilla, lemon rind and cinnamon. Add just enough hot milk to make a smooth sauce. Taste for seasoning.

3 Drain fusilli and toss through ricotta sauce. Serve immediately, decorated with lemon rind and sprinkled with cinnamon.

SERVES 4

PASTA WITH FRUIT AND NUTS

⅔ pound rigatoni or other large, hollow tubes

3 ounces dried figs, softened in boiling
water 15 minutes and finely chopped

½ cup toasted blanched almonds, finely chopped

½ cup walnuts, finely chopped

¼ cup raisins, chopped

3 tablespoons marmalade

grated rind 1 large orange

pinch ground cloves

¼ teaspoon cinnamon

6 tablespoons butter, melted and browned

sugar

vanilla ice cream, softened

1 Preheat oven to 375°F.

2 Cook rigatoni in boiling salted water until
just *al dente*. Drain, rinse under cold water
and drain again. Stir through a little
vegetable oil and set aside.

3 In a bowl combine figs, almonds, walnuts,
raisins, marmalade, orange rind and spices
and mix well. Stuff each pasta tube with
filling (use a pastry bag with a large nozzle).
Place in a single layer in a buttered, shallow
ovenproof dish. Pour over butter, sprinkle
with sugar and bake for 10 to 14 minutes.
Serve immediately with softened ice cream.

SERVES 4

ALMOND TORTE

4 cups milk

1 cup sugar

1 cup risoni

3 tablespoons vanilla

1 cup blanched almonds

2 tablespoons extra sugar

1 tablespoon dried breadcrumbs

6 eggs

¼ cup almond liqueur

1 teaspoon almond extract

1 In a large saucepan combine milk with
sugar, and bring to the boil. Add risoni and

1 tablespoon vanilla and boil for 10 minutes,
stirring once to twice. Set aside.

2 Preheat oven to 300°F.

3 Put almonds close together on a sheet of
foil on a baking tray. Sprinkle with the extra
sugar and some water and place under a hot
broiler until caramelised. Chop coarsely with
breadcrumbs in a food processor or by hand.

4 Beat eggs, almond liqueur and extract,
and remaining vanilla together. Add risoni
mixture and almonds and mix well. Pour
into a buttered 10-inch baking dish and
bake for about 1 hour, or until the top is
golden brown and the torte set.

5 Remove from the oven and immediately
prick holes over the entire surface with a
toothpick or skewer. Sprinkle generously
with additional almond liqueur and let cool.

SERVES 6 TO 8

Almond Torte

Preparing Sweet Ravioli

VILLA ITALIANA

4 Preheat oven to 350°F.

5 Working one sheet at a time, place half teaspoons of jam at evenly spaced intervals along and across its length. Paint between the jam along the cutting lines with beaten egg. Cover this sheet with another one and run along the cutting lines with your finger to seal the two sides together. Cut out the ravioli with a floured fluted pastry wheel. Repeat with the remaining sheets of pasta.

6 Brush the ravioli with beaten egg and place on a buttered baking tray. Bake until crisp and golden, about 30 minutes. Cool slightly and serve dusted with confectioner's sugar.

SERVES 4

SWEET RAVIOLI

1 cup sifted potato flour

1 ¼ cups sifted flour

pinch salt

½ cup sugar

4 tablespoons butter

1 egg

grated rind 1 lemon

3 tablespoons milk

thick jam for filling

beaten egg for sealing

≈ SWEET RAVIOLI VARIATIONS

These ravioli can be served as a dessert with cream or mascarpone, or alone with coffee. They can also be deep-fried instead of baked, in which case they have a crisper pastry, but don't keep. If deep-frying, omit brushing the ravioli with beaten egg.

1 To make the pasta by hand, sift flours, salt and sugar together and then cut in the butter. Add remaining ingredients except jam and mix to form a dry but pliable dough, using a little more milk or extra flour if needed. Cover and rest for 1 hour.

2 If using a food processor, mix dry ingredients briefly (using the metal blade) and then add butter and egg. Mix for a couple of seconds before adding the rest of the ingredients and continue processing until the dough forms a ball and slows or stops the machine. Rest for 1 hour, covered.

3 Divide dough into quarters, then roll out each piece into a very thin sheet about 12 inches long. Cover with plastic wrap or a damp towel.

SWEET CHEESE IN LEMON PASTA

These lemon packets can be prepared earlier in the day and kept in the refrigerator, loosely covered, until ready to cook. Experiment with the size and shape of them; they look very good made smaller in a more traditional ravioli size.

PASTA

2 ½ cups sifted flour

½ teaspoon salt

1 teaspoon sugar

grated rind 2 lemons

3 tablespoons fresh lemon juice

1 small egg, beaten

FILLING

1 ½ pounds cottage cheese

⅔ cup sugar

¾ cup candied lemon peel

3 ounces dark chocolate, grated

½ teaspoon vanilla

1 tablespoon brandy

TO ASSEMBLE

beaten egg for sealing

vegetable oil for frying

1 cup heavy cream, flavored to taste with brandy

caster sugar

1 TO PREPARE PASTA: Pile flour, salt, sugar and lemon rind on a work surface and make a well in the center. Add lemon juice and egg and begin blending them into the flour, using a fork. When a loosely combined dough is obtained, use your hands and knead it, incorporating extra flour as you go to form a smooth, elastic ball. Cover with a damp cloth or plastic wrap and rest for 15 minutes.
2 Divide the ball into four and, working one-quarter at a time, roll each into a very thin sheet, and cover each as it is completed. Rest again while you are preparing the filling.
3 TO PREPARE FILLING: Combine all ingredients thoroughly.

4 Cut pasta into 7-inch squares. Working a few at a time, brush round the edges of each pasta square with a little beaten egg. Place some filling in the middle of each and fold it in, like an envelope, to completely enclose. Press the edges down to seal tightly.
5 Heat a ½-inch or so of oil in a pan until a slight haze is formed. Fry pasta packets, one or two at a time, until golden on both sides. Remove with a slotted spoon and drain on absorbent paper, keep warm while the remainder are cooking.
Serve warm with brandy cream and sprinkled with sugar.

SERVES 4 TO 6

Sweet Cheese in Lemon Pasta

≈ CHOCOLATE
FETTUCCINE WITH
ORANGE BUTTER

*This dish is
embarrassingly easy but
is always a show stopper
when served at the finale
of a dinner party. The
pasta can be prepared
earlier in the day and
kept moist, and the
orange can be grated
beforehand as well.*

≈ FARFALLE WITH
PISTACHIOS

*This is rich and delicate
and so easy to make.
Sauté 1 cup of pistachios
in ¼ pound melted butter
until golden. Add
3 tablespoons poppy seeds
and 1 tablespoon sugar
and stir to coat. Toss
through ½ pound cooked
farfalle .*

CHOCOLATE FETTUCCINE WITH ORANGE BUTTER

CHOCOLATE PASTA

1½ cups semolina, durum wheat if possible

1 cup sifted flour

1 tablespoon sweetened powdered chocolate

1 teaspoon cocoa powder

pinch salt

1 egg, lightly beaten

1 teaspoon vegetable oil

ORANGE BUTTER

10 tablespoons (1¼ sticks) unsalted butter

1 large orange

1 TO PREPARE PASTA: Sift dry ingredients together. Gradually mix in egg and oil, adding a little water if necessary, to form a dry but well-combined dough. (Alternatively, dough can be mixed in a food processor.) Knead on a lightly floured board for 6 to 7 minutes to give a smooth and elastic ball. Rest for at least 15 minutes.

2 Divide dough in two and roll each half out into a thin rectangular sheet roughly 8 inches long. Let the pasta sit for a few minutes before cutting. Either cut the sheets into fettuccine using a pasta machine, or roll each up along its length and slice off the ribbons with a sharp knife.

3 Cook the pasta in boiling salted water.

4 TO PREPARE ORANGE BUTTER: Peel rind off one-quarter of the orange, remove any pith left on the rind and slice it very thinly into 1-inch lengths. With a very fine grater, grate the zest off the rest of the orange, being careful not to collect any of the pith.

5 In a small saucepan heat butter until it browns slightly. If the butter fats begin to separate, strain the butter into another saucepan and proceed. Add orange rind and zest. Heat gently for 2 to 3 minutes until orange rind gives off its distinctive aroma.

6 Drain cooked pasta and quickly pour the sauce over it. Serve immediately with lightly whipped cream or mascarpone.

SERVES 4

CHOCOLATE NUT CAKE

½ pound farfalle

1 cup roasted hazelnuts

1½ cups walnut halves

¾ cup blanched almonds

3 tablespoons dried breadcrumbs

4 tablespoons cocoa powder

3 tablespoons dark chocolate, grated

1 teaspoon cinnamon

⅔ cup sugar

1½ tablespoons mixed peel, finely chopped

grated rind 1 lemon

1 teaspoon vanilla

4 tablespoons cognac

1 Cook pasta in boiling salted water to which has been added a teaspoon of sugar. When it is barely done, drain.

2 Chop nuts and breadcrumbs together in a food processor until a coarse paste forms. Transfer to a bowl and mix with the rest of the ingredients. Stir about ½ cup of this mixture through the warm pasta.

3 In a buttered deep round casserole spread a thin layer of nut paste. Cover this with a layer of pasta, then another of the paste, continuing until fillings are used up. Finish with a topping of nut paste. Cover cake with a flat plate just big enough to fit into the dish, and press down well. Store in a cool spot or refrigerate for at least 12 hours, pressing on the plate from time to time.

4 Serve at room temperature and decorate with some extra grated chocolate or a dusting of confectioner's sugar. Cut the cake into wedges while still in the dish. Serve with coffee or as a dessert with whipped cream.

MAKES 12 TO 16 SLICES

INDEX